OUR PRESIDENTS & THEIR PRAYERS

Proclamations of Faith by America's Leaders

by Senator Rand Paul

Compiled and Edited by James Randall Robison

CENTER STREET

New York Boston Nashville

You are the light of the world. A town built on a hill cannot be hidden. . . . let your light shine before others, that they may see your good deeds and glorify your Father in heaven.

—Matthew 5:14

For additional credits, permissions, and sources see page 159.

CENTER STREET
Hachette Book Group
1290 Avenue of the Americas
New York, NY 10104

www.CenterStreet.com

Photo Editor Christopher Measom *Book design by Timothy Shaner*

Printed in the United States of America

WOR

First edition: October 2015

10 9 8 7 6 5 4 3 2 1

Center Street is a division of Hachette Book Group, Inc.
The Center Street name and logo are trademarks of Hachette Book Group, Inc.

Library of Congress Control Number: 2015947666

ISBNs: 978-1-4555-3573-6 (hardcover ed.), 978-1-4555-3849-2 (reg. autographed ed.), 978-1-4555-3848-5 (B&N autographed ed.)

Pilgrim fathers arriving in America.

EACH ACCORDING TO THE DICTATES
OF HIS OWN CONSCIENCE

Introduction

Americans often take for granted that our country was born of a religious people. We sometimes discount the importance of religion as the stabilizing force that allowed us to proceed in relative calm from the chaos of war to an enduring nation guided by faith and the rule of law.

One of the media's favorite questions to politicians is: "Do you believe America is a Christian nation?" Well, it is of course a historical fact that we were founded by a religious people, most of whom were Christians. But if one tries to expound on that point, even to acknowledge its historical significance, some immediately want to paint you as an intolerant believer in theocracy.

The media so often dumbs down the debate that the general public fails to appreciate how uniquely fortunate we were that our American Revolution was the exception to the rule played out repeatedly in world history—bloodshed, violence, and enduring chaos.

Among revolutions, America's was extraordinary in that once we threw off the yoke of the king, we didn't also cast off our traditions. We kept our religious faith. We maintained a thousand year history of English common law. We considered our revolution to be a continuation and natural progression of the battle for individual rights that began at Runnymede in 1215.

Consider, for example, how the American Revolution differed dramatically from the French Revolution.

In America, we fought to be free of the British King but we maintained our several hundred year tradition of limited governmental power and we kept our bedrock religious faith. We didn't forget or attempt to turn away from the quest for individual rights that began with the Magna Carta. We built upon its keystone. Our founders were not bashful in acknowledging God's Grace in our history.

Freedom of Worship *by Norman Rockwell, 1943.*

Contrast that with the French Revolution, where the king and religion were to a degree inseparable and rejected simultaneously. As a result, violent chaos and destruction ensued.

The American Revolution was also extraordinary in that it gave birth to the first real meritocracy. Barbara Tuchman writes of how novel it was that the American Revolution opened up progress to people from all walks of life, not just the nobility.

While it took awhile for the Republic to include everyone, the fact that it occurred and remains is, to my mind, nothing short of a miracle.

Some modern critics worry though that we do not separate religion from government enough. They seek to not only divide faith from our government but also from the private sector businesses of our citizens. They argue that the Christian owners of Hobby Lobby should be forced by law to keep their faith out of their business.

But when the US Government decreed that Hobby Lobby would be forced to purchase insurance covering procedures its owners found morally objectionable, they responded, unbowed, in a way that speaks to the core of America's founding principles. Their lawyer wrote:

"Obamacare asks us to abandon our faith to remain in business or abandon our business to remain true to our faith."

In a free country, such a question should be unthinkable. Such a question is inconsistent with liberty. Indeed, such a question is antithetical to the American tradition.

Modern day pundits act as if the separation of church and state means that our origins were based upon a purely secular state devoid of the influence of religion.

Nothing could be further from the truth. To a person, all of our Presidents have acknowledged the guiding influence of their faith.

Today's critics sometimes imply that you can't have both faith and freedom. Some think you must choose between faith or freedom, or put a different way—liberty or virtue.

I disagree.

I believe that liberty is absolutely essential to virtue, and vice versa. After all, it is the freedom to make individual choices that allows us to be virtuous.

Don Devine gets to the heart of the matter in his book, *America's Way Back*. He writes:

"Freedom needs tradition for law, order, inspiration.

Tradition needs freedom to escape stagnation, coercion, and decline.

The great achievement of the Constitution's framers was in providing a means for synthesizing freedom and tradition."

Government can't impose virtue, we must impose it on ourselves.

Government can't provide salvation, only the individual can choose to be saved.

Government can supply bread, but it can't mend a broken spirit.

To paraphrase Os Guiness, "Liberty requires restraint but the only restraint consistent with liberty is voluntary restraint."

This does not mean government cannot or should not reflect our values. In fact, it must. I believe that leaders guided by faith, leaders guided by virtue, are essential.

Most of our Presidents recognized this principle, especially President Washington. He recognized that freedom requires an undergirding of faith. Washington believed that democracy depended upon a virtuous people. His prayers and writings, and those of the other great Presidents in our history contained in these pages, reveal how integral our religious traditions were to our founding, and I believe, to our future as well.

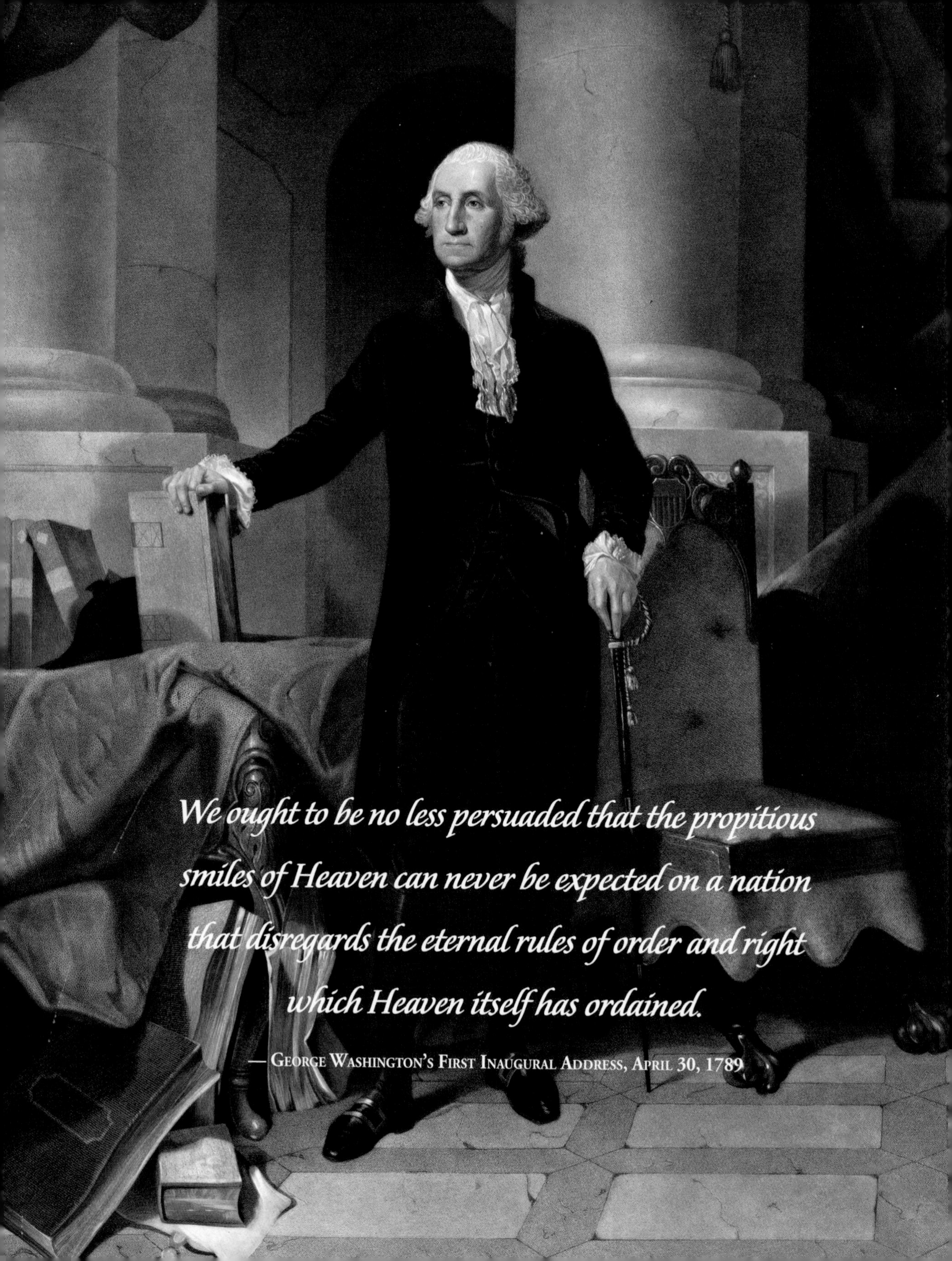

We ought to be no less persuaded that the propitious smiles of Heaven can never be expected on a nation that disregards the eternal rules of order and right which Heaven itself has ordained.

— George Washington's First Inaugural Address, April 30, 1789

1ST

GEORGE WASHINGTON

1789-1797

LET THE WORLD BE FILLED WITH THE KNOWLEDGE OF THEE AND THY SON JESUS CHRIST.

From his election as Commander in Chief of the Continental Army to the end of his second term as president, George Washington stood as the quintessential American leader. After the ratification of the U.S. Constitution, he was unanimously elected as our nation's first president. On April 30, 1789, he placed his hand on an open Bible while standing on the balcony of Federal Hall in New York City. After taking the oath, church bells rang out across the city as the crowd thundered with applause. President Washington then delivered the first inaugural address to Congress, which included a patent acknowledgement of God's hand in the establishment of a new, free land.

I now make it my earnest prayer that God would have you, and the State over which you preside, in his holy protection; that he would incline the hearts of the citizens to cultivate a spirit of subordination and obedience to government, to entertain a brotherly affection and love for one another, for their fellow-citizens of the United States at large, and particularly for brethren who have served in the field; and finally that he would most graciously be pleased to dispose us all to do justice, to love mercy,

Ingraving of George Washington by Alexander H. Ritchie, 1852 based on a painting by Peter Frederick Rothermel.

FIRST INAUGURAL ADDRESS
April 30, 1789

It would be peculiarly improper to omit, in this first official act, my fervent supplications to that Almighty Being who rules over the universe, who presides in the councils of nations and whose providential aide can supply every human defect, that His benediction may consecrate to the liberties and happiness of the people of the United States a Government instituted by themselves for these essential purposes; and may enable every instrument employed in its administration to execute with success, the functions allotted to his charge.

In tendering this homage to the Great Author of every public and private good, I assure myself that it expresses your sentiments not less than my own; nor those of my fellow-citizens at large, less than either. No people can be bound to acknowledge and adore the Invisible Hand which conducts the affairs of men more than the people of the United States.

Washington praying in the snow at Valley Forge by Frederick Heppenheimer, 1876.

and to demean ourselves with that charity, humility, and pacific temper of mind, which were the characteristics of the Divine Author of our blessed religion, and without an humble imitation of whose example in these things, we can never hope to be a happy nation.

—Circular Letter Addressed to the Governors of all the States
June 8, 1783

Let me live according to those holy rules which thou hast this day prescribed in thy holy word; make me to know what is acceptable in thy holy word; make me to know what is acceptable in thy sight, and therein to delight, open the eyes of my understanding, and help me thoroughly to examine myself concerning my knowledge, faith and repentance, increase my faith, and direct me to the true object Jesus Christ the way, the truth and the life, bless O Lord, all the people of this land, from the highest to the lowest, particularly those whom thou has appointed to rule over us in church and state. Continue thy goodness to me this night. These weak petitions I humbly implore thee to hear accept and answer for the sake of thy Dear Son Jesus Christ our Lord. Amen.

—George Washington's Prayer Journal, Sunday Evening Prayer

Washington's reputation as a general went hand in hand with his renown as a man of faith. He sought God's intervention as he fought for freedom. And when the war was at its lowest ebb he sought solace on his knees before God at Valley Forge.

Brueckner's portrait of Washington in prayer continues to inspire. In fact, Reagan said that the portrait of George Washington kneeling in the snow praying at Valley Forge "personified a people who knew it was not enough to depend on their own courage and goodness; they must also seek help from God, their Father and their Preserver."

In the bitter cold winter of 1777 at Valley Forge, General Washington bent his knee in prayer.

Like so many stories surrounding Washington it is sometimes hard to sort out the apocryphal from fact. But the story recounted by Isaac Potts, a young Quaker resident of Valley Forge, appears consistent with what we know of Washington's faith. Potts had firsthand knowledge. He was there at Valley Forge overseeing the grinding of grain for the army.

Potts' story is recounted in the "Diary and Remembrances" of Rev. Nathaniel Randolph Snowden, a Presbyterian minister and a Princeton graduate (Original Manuscript at the Historical Society of Pennsylvania; Call no. PHi.Am.1561-1568).

> *"I was riding with him (Mr. Potts) near Valley Forge, where the army lay during the war of the Revolution. Mr. Potts was a Senator in our state and a Whig. I told him I was agreeably surprised to find him a friend to his country as the Quakers were mostly Tories. He said, "It was so and I was a rank Tory once, for I never believed that America could proceed against Great Britain whose fleets and armies covered the land and ocean. But something very extraordinary converted me to the good faith."*
>
> *"What was that?" I inquired. "Do you see that woods, and that plain?" It was about a quarter of a mile from the place we were riding. "There," said he, "laid the army of Washington. It was a most distressing time of ye war, and all were for giving up the ship but that one good man. In that woods," pointing to a close in view, "I heard a plaintive sound, as of a man at prayer. I tied my horse to a sapling and went quietly into the woods and to my astonishment I saw the great George Washington on his knees alone, with his sword on one side and his cocked hat on the other. He was at Prayer to the God of the Armies, beseeching to interpose with his Divine aid, as it was ye Crisis and the cause of the country, of humanity, and of the world.*
>
> *"Such a prayer I never heard from the lips of man. I left him alone praying. I went home and told my wife, 'I saw a sight and heard today what I never saw or heard before', and just related to her what I had seen and heard and observed. We never thought a man could be a soldier and a Christian, but if there is one in the world, it is Washington. We thought it was the cause of God, and America could prevail."*

One of the things I am most grateful for in my life is that I was blessed to be born into a large and loving family, with two wonderful parents. Together with our spouses, my four siblings, and I have nineteen kids between us. With six married or engaged, there are now twenty-five in that generation, with seven great-grandchildren also in the mix. Typically, there are over forty people at dinners of "just the family. " I love it.

There is a special strength and comfort in knowing that there are so many people who stand with you and behind you—no matter what unfolds in your life. I was reminded of that again just recently, as my mother and younger sister Joy hosted events in Texas to celebrate my wife Kelley's new book, *True and Constant Friends.*

My mother Carol hosted an afternoon tea and my sisters, sisters-in-law and nieces all helped with every detail—flowers, food, invitations and decor. Kelley was so touched by the labor of love. Our niece Vicki sang "God Bless America" a capella, to begin one of the events, and did so having been given virtually no advance warning! That's the way my family is: always ready to do what is asked.

My sister Joy is a busy OB-GYN and a mother of six, the youngest of whom is only two, but she had the time and energy to host a luncheon for nearly two hundred people who came out to hear Kelley speak. Many members of Joy's church were there, including her pastor and his wife.

Kelley and I were so moved by the outpouring of prayers and encouragement we received from Joy's church family, people we had never met before. Many of the guests were also Joy's patients—the fathers and mothers of the thousands of babies she has delivered. One of the guests, a longtime patient of Joy's, said to me that day, "Your parents sure knew what they were doing when they named your sister Joy." That is certainly true.

Our first president spoke of the "Great Author" of all that is good. When I think of my family, and the values and faith they hold dear, I think of the benevolence of His almighty pen. I look at my family and I'm grateful for the bountiful love He has scripted for me.

2ND

JOHN ADAMS

1797-1801

I PRAY HEAVEN TO BESTOW THE BEST OF BLESSINGS ON THIS HOUSE AND ALL THAT SHALL HEREAFTER INHABIT IT. MAY NONE BUT HONEST AND WISE MEN EVER RULE UNDER THIS ROOF.

John Adams was our nation's first Vice President, serving both terms under President Washington. He was a Harvard-educated lawyer, a delegate to the First and Second Continental Congresses, a signer of the Declaration of Independence, and a diplomat to France and Holland during the American Revolution.

Although his religious views were unorthodox and ever evolving, he held to a belief in God and, in the words of his grandson Charles Francis Adams, "he was content to settle down upon the Sermon on the Mount as a perfect code presented to men by a more than mortal teacher."

What I have always loved about John Adams and really his entire clan is that they lived out their religious beliefs. In a time in which much was excused, in a time in which many leaders failed to condemn slavery, the Adamses rose above the norms of the day to be a voice against the it.

John Adams *by Gilbert Stuart c. 1800.*

His opposition to slavery was not loud enough during the Constitutional Convention to prevent the loathsome practice from continuing, but nevertheless his opposition was well known and Adams was always proud of his position against human bondage.

Adams' views are quite clear in his letter to Robert I. Evans, June, 1819:

> *"Every measure of prudence, therefore, ought to be assumed for the eventual total extirpation of slavery from the United States.*
>
> *"I have, through my whole life, held the practice of slavery in such abhorrence, that I have never owned a negro or any other slave; though I have lived for many years in times when the practice was not disgraceful; when the best men in my vicinity thought it not inconsistent with their character; and when it has cost me thousands of dollars of the labor and subsistence of free men . . ."*
>
> —*Works of John Adams*

In his inaugural address, Adams acknowledges that the fate of the Republic and the success of the country rely upon and are necessarily intertwined with the benevolence of our Creator.

I do hereby recommend accordingly, that Thursday, the 25th day of April next, be observed throughout the United States of America as a day of solemn humiliation, fasting, and prayer; that the citizens on that day abstain as far as may be from their secular occupations, devote the time to the sacred duties of religion in public and in private; that they call to mind our numerous offenses against the Most High God, confess them before Him with the sincerest penitence, implore His pardoning mercy, through the Great Mediator and Redeemer, for our past transgressions, and that through the grace of His Holy Spirit we may be disposed and enabled to yield a more suitable obedience to His righteous requisitions in time to come.

—Presidential Proclamation, March 6, 1799

Perhaps most poignant among Adams' letters was one he wrote to Thomas Jefferson, his friend and political rival, shortly after the death of his wife Abigail. In mourning the loss of his beloved, he meditates on God, human love, and the afterlife:

INAUGURAL ADDRESS
March 4, 1797

With humble reverence, I feel it to be my duty to add, if a veneration for the religion of a people who profess and call themselves Christians, and a fixed resolution to consider a decent respect for Christianity among the best recommendations for the public service, can enable me in any degree to comply with your wishes, it shall be my strenuous endeavor that this sagacious injunction of the two Houses shall not be without effect.

With this great example before me, with the sense and spirit, the faith and honor, the duty and interest, of the same American people pledged to support the Constitution of the United States, I entertain no doubt of its continuance in all its energy, and my mind is prepared without hesitation to lay myself under the most solemn obligations to support it to the utmost of my power.

And may that Being who is supreme over all, the Patron of Order, the Fountain of Justice, and the Protector in all ages of the world of virtuous liberty, continue His blessing upon this nation and its Government and give it all possible success and duration consistent with the ends of His providence.

The First Prayer in Congress, September 7th, 1774, in Carpenters Hall, Philadelphia, mezzotint 1848.

"I do not know how to prove, physically, that we shall meet and know each other in a future state; nor does revelation, as I can find, give us any positive assurance of such a felicity. My reasons for believing it, as I do most undoubtedly, are that I cannot conceive such a being could make such a species as the human, merely to live and die on this earth. If I did not believe in a future state, I should believe in no God. This universe, this all would appear, with all of its swelling pomp, a boyish firework. And if there be a future state, why should the Almighty dissolve forever all the tender ties which unite us so delightfully in this world, and forbid us to see each other in the next?"

His anguished, yet still hopeful question reminds me of one of my favorite spiritual songs, *The Wayfaring Stranger*, an American folk classic. I'll never forget how moved I was hearing a woman sing it accompanied by a mandolin and guitar at our church in Bowling Green one morning. Its plaintive words and melody speak to the yearnings of the human heart for love and peace, and the desire to see the faces of our loved ones who've gone before, "God's redeemed, their vigils keep."

I'm just a poor wayfaring stranger
Traveling through this world of woe
There's no sickness, toil nor danger
In that fair land to which I go
I'm going there to see my father
I'm going there no more to roam
I'm just a-going over Jordan
I'm just a-going over home

I know dark clouds will hover o'er me
I know my path way is rough and steep
But golden fields lie out before me
Where God's redeemed their vigils keep
I'm going there to see my mother
She said she'd meet me when I come
I'm only going over Jordan
I'm only going over home

I'll soon be free, from every trial
This form shall rest beneath the sun
I'll drop the cross of self-denial
And enter in the home with God.
I'm going there to see my Saviour
I'm going home no more to roam
I'm just a-going over Jordan
I'm just a-going over home

3RD

THOMAS JEFFERSON

1801–1809

MAY THAT INFINITE POWER WHICH RULES THE DESTINIES OF THE UNIVERSE LEAD OUR COUNCILS . . .

Thomas Jefferson's greatest contribution to the United States came at the birth of the new nation when he penned the Declaration of Independence. His argument that "all men are created equal, that they are endowed by their Creator with certain unalienable Rights" provided the foundation for a Constitution that derived its authority not from a king, elected representative, or popular majority, but from God Himself.

His early efforts to legally establish religious freedom in the state of Virginia foreshadowed his dedication to every individual's right to worship without government interference. His letter responding to the complaints of government encroachment by the Baptists in Danbury, Connecticut, pledged his support for their freedoms, and his inaugural addresses reflected his personal reverence for the One who granted his very right to govern.

Bless our land with honorable industry, sound learning and pure manners. Save us from violence, discord and confusion; from pride and arrogance, and from every evil way. Defend our liberties and fashion into one united people the multitudes brought hither out of many kindreds and tongues. Endow with the spirit of wisdom those to whom in thy name we entrust the authority of government, that there may be justice and peace at home, and that through obedience to thy law, we may show forth thy praise among the nations of the earth. In the time of prosperity, fill our hearts with thankfulness, and in days of trouble, suffer not our trust in thee to fail; all of which we ask through our Lord. Amen.

—Thomas Jefferson's "Prayer For The Nation"
Air Force Chaplain Corps Book of Prayers

Believing with you that religion is a matter which lies solely between Man & his God, that he owes account to none other for his faith or his worship, that the legitimate powers of government reach actions only, & not opinions, I contemplate with sovereign reverence that act of the whole American people which declared that their legislature should "make no law respecting an establishment of religion, or prohibiting the free exercise thereof," thus building a wall of separation between Church & State. Adhering to this expression of the supreme will of the nation in behalf of the rights of conscience, I shall see with sincere satisfaction the progress of those sentiments which tend to restore to man all his natural rights, convinced he has no natural right in opposition to his social duties.

—Letter to the Danbury Baptists, January 1, 1802

Jefferson is unique among Presidents in that he "created" an abridged Bible that some still refer to as the Jefferson Bible. He chose to include only the words directly attributable to Jesus. Some say Jefferson was a Deist. Deism views God not so much as existing before the creation but as a consequence of witnessing what was created. Whatever the conclusion, he was a man who greatly respected the teachings of Jesus and it would be wrong to assert that Jefferson was not a man of great faith.

Jefferson is given credit for initiating the concept of separation of church and state in the letter to the Danbury Baptists quoted above. But I don't think he would have ever imagined that one day people would advocate for a separation that forbade religious people from expressing their faith in office, or in their private sector businesses.

I also don't think Jefferson could have imagined how easy the act of war has become for us. Without question our founders understood the horror of the endless wars of Europe—wars fought among the royal cousins mostly for reasons undecipherable by the soldiers who fought them, who were mere pawns on a chessboard.

Our founders desperately wanted to make war difficult to initiate. And with great precision they gave the power of initiating war to the legislature not the President.

Jefferson, in a letter to Madison, makes this point: "We have already given in example one effectual check to the dog of war by transferring the power of letting him loose from the Executive to the Legislative body. . . ."

Every generation of war has one noble soul who records the devastation of combat. WWI had Wilfred Owen. He was a poet and a soldier in WWI. While all war has its moments of horror, WWI overflowed with gore and senseless death, made even more terrible by the seemingly inexplicable reasons for the war, reasons the working class soldiers could likely not conceive of even as they were asked to fight and die. Owen captured the despair and the false patriotism that sent young men to their death in his poem "Dulce et Decorum Est."

If you could hear, at every jolt, the blood
come gargling from the froth-corrupted lungs,
obscene as cancer, bitter as the cud
of vile, incurable sores on innocent tongues—
My friend, you would not tell with such high jest
To children ardent for some desperate glory,
The old Lie:
Dulce et decorum est
Pro patria mori.
(sweet and fitting it is to die for one's country)

I'm reminded of the schoolmaster in Erich Maria Remarque's *All Quiet on the Western Front* who exhorted the young men to enlist for the fatherland with tales of bravery and battlefield fame. When the schoolchildren came home maimed and shell-shocked, they avoided him like the plague. They now understood that war was no fairy tale.

Historically, wars were fought by everyone except for the select few who could buy their non-participation. But the vast majority of the population fought. Over the past two decades of war, though, only a small number of families have borne the brunt of our decades long war in the Middle East.

Detail of View of the West Front of Monticello and Garden *by Jane Braddick Peticolas, 1825.*

In the poem below, I imagine the point of view from the non-soldier class, those who see war as a game played on a video screen because they don't have to participate. I sometimes fear that is the view of some of our politicians who too easily glorify and engage us in war. This perspective glimpses the gore and horror of war yet crassly avoids doing anything to stop it—as long as there is "sufficient unwashed" to carry on the fight.

When war came most were incredulous
To think that Mario could be asked to pause
That Zelda might wait while bullets need penetrate spines
And metal might fragment dreams and brains and limbs
Most inconvenient said many if not all
That war might come to us all

Better some said to let the masses amass and make no mention of motions
of muscles that might sprain or tear or avulse
better to expose prose and propose proposals of the highest patriotic praise
That Certain select and sensible, valuable souls remain
rested and refined for finery and phrase

for war, that pesky thing, that seemingly arises
erect—of its own mind
for nary a cause
is surely not the thing for manicured hands

But war it seems came
Pause and rewind did not protect the protected
When limb strewn from limb exposed the wan, untanned
but properly washed
To a stew comprised of brain and butchered brawn
the good people protested as much

Why must we sacrifice our best and our brightest
are there not sufficient unwashed?

—Rand Paul

4TH

JAMES MADISON

1809–1817

. . . TO THE GOODNESS OF A SUPERINTENDING PROVIDENCE, TO WHICH WE ARE INDEBTED . . .

Often called the "Father of the Constitution," James Madison influenced the formation of the country through his service in the Continental Congress, the Virginia Assembly, and his essays in the Federalist Papers. While an Assemblyman, he successfully argued that the Virginia Declaration of Rights should not merely express religious "toleration," but should be amended to guarantee "free exercise of religion, according to the dictates of conscience." Madison went on to serve in the first four Congresses of the United States, where he helped frame the Bill of Rights. Thomas Jefferson promoted him to Secretary of State, then endorsed him for president when he chose not to run for a third term.

Madison is one of my favorite presidents because he was one of the primary authors of the Constitution and the Bill of Rights. His explanation of the Constitution in the Federalist Papers continues to guide us in understanding the intentions of the founders.

Two of my favorite Madison quotes are:

> *"The constitution supposes, what the History of all Governments demonstrates, that the Executive is the branch of power most interested in war, and most prone to it. It has accordingly with studied care vested the question of war to the Legis-*

> *lature." (Letter to Jefferson, c. 1798.)* and *" If men were angels, no government would be necessary. If angels were to govern men, neither external nor internal controls on government would be necessary." (Federalist No. 51)*

In 2013, during my thirteen hour filibuster I repeatedly quoted Madison's admonition that government must be restrained because we are never governed by angels.

I believe that one of President Obama's greatest failings is that he recognizes the inherent danger in allowing American citizens to be detained without trial but then justifies his decision to sign such legislation by averring, "But I am a good man and I would never use such a power."

Laws are not written to restrain "good men." Laws are written acknowledging that government is not always led by "good men." This erroneous understanding leads to a greater and greater governmental control of our lives. My first filibuster, though superficially about drones, was really about due process, about protecting the individual's presumption of innocence.

In the spring of 2015, I took to the floor of the Senate proudly wearing my James Madison tie to wage a new filibuster against the government's bulk collection of phone records. Some say what's the big deal? They're only boring old business records. Those of

FIRST INAUGURAL ADDRESS
March 4, 1809

But the source to which I look or the aids which alone can supply my deficiencies is in the well-tried intelligence and virtue of my fellow-citizens, and in the counsels of those representing them in the other departments associated in the care of the national interests. In these my confidence will under every difficulty be best placed, next to that which we have all been encouraged to feel in the guardianship and guidance of that Almighty Being whose power regulates the destiny of nations, whose blessings have been so conspicuously dispensed to this rising Republic, and to whom we are bound to address our devout gratitude for the past, as well as our fervent supplications and best hopes for the future.

us who defend privacy understand that from phone records you can determine someone's religion, someone's doctor, and someone's associations the vast majority of the time. I think Madison would be proud that someone still cares enough about the Bill of Rights, specifically the fourth amendment, to stand on the Senate floor for nearly 11 hours.

Madison was there when George Mason refused to support the Constitution because it didn't have a Bill of Rights. Madison was there when John Adams argued that the spark that led to the War for Independence was sparked by James Otis' fight against general warrants.

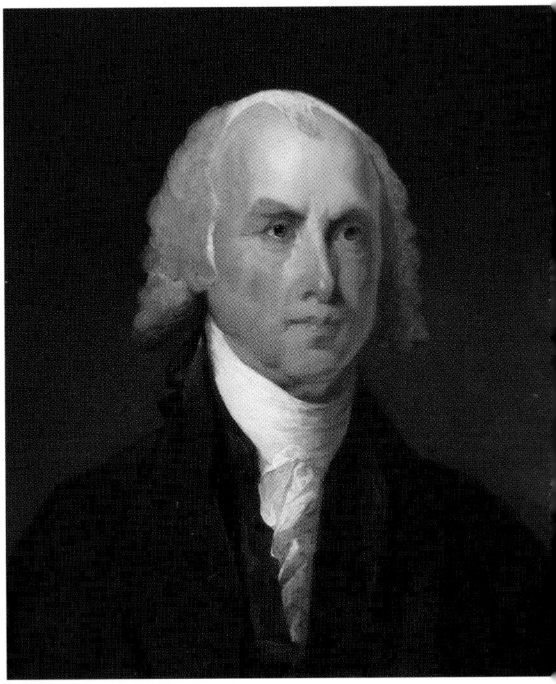

My filibuster against bulk collection of phone records was really a filibuster in defense of the fourth amendment that insists that warrants be individualized and supported by probable cause that an individual has committed a crime.

Collecting all American phone records all the time is hardly individualized and is in no way related to suspicion of any kind. Madison, and likely all of the founding fathers, would be aghast to see this dishonoring of the fourth amendment.

After ten and half hours of filibuster against the Patriot Act and against bulk collection of records, I succeeded in making it past midnight and pushing the debate into Memorial Day weekend. Some colleagues were unamused and bashed me in the media for having the presumption to filibuster in defense of the fourth amendment.

As I stood hour after hour wearing my Madison tie, I imagined Madison smiling his approval.

Some in the media insinuated that my filibuster won nothing. I disagree. Before my filibuster began there were only 57 votes to end the President's illegal, generalized collection of all of our phone records. For one reason or another, perhaps simply piqued at my disrupting the apple cart, ten Senators changed their votes after my filibuster to vote against the illegal bulk collection of records.

James Madison *by Gilbert Sutart c. 1821.*

Some say that night I lost any chance to become President. Who knows. My critics were legion and they wrote and rewrote my obituary all night long.

That night, I defended the essence of what makes us exceptional, what Justice Brandeis once said was the most cherished of rights—the right to be left alone.

I remain honored to have stood on the Senate floor and given my best to defend the right to be left alone.

Madison, like most of the founders, knew that the Constitution needed to bind the government and restrict the accumulation of power.

Unfortunately, over time, the Supreme Court and our politicians have paid less and less attention to Madison and power has grown and grown and gravitated into the hands of the Executive. So much power has devolved to the President that Congress has become almost impotent and ineffectual.

In the prayers below, Madison references his belief in the "intelligence and virtue" of the people and seeks the guidance of the Almighty.

It is impossible for any man of candor to reflect on this circumstance without partaking of the astonishment. It is impossible for the man of pious reflection not to perceive in it a finger of that Almighty hand which has been so frequently and signally extended to our relief in the critical stages of the revolution.

—The Federalist No. 37, January 11, 1788

Recollecting always that for every advantage which may contribute to distinguish our lot from that to which others are doomed by the unhappy spirit of the times, we are indebted to that Divine Providence whose goodness has been so remarkably extended to this rising nation; it becomes us to cherish a devout gratitude, and to implore from the same omnipotent source a blessing on the consultations and measures about to be undertaken for the welfare of our beloved country.

—First Annual Message, November 29, 1809

5TH

JAMES MONROE

1817-1825

. . . WITH A FIRM RELIANCE ON THE PROTECTION OF ALMIGHTY GOD . . .

James Monroe first rose to prominence as a Major in the Continental Army. After resigning his commission, he served as a United States Senator and the Minister to France during Washington's presidency. He later served multiple terms as the governor of Virginia. He was also tapped by Madison as Secretary of State and then Secretary of War. When Madison decided not to run in 1816, he endorsed Monroe.

Early in his first term, a Boston newspaper declared him the "Era-of-Good-Feeling President." His policies in foreign affairs, dubbed the Monroe Doctrine, shaped the future for decades and helped prevent encroachment by Russia and European powers in the Western Hemisphere.

When, then, we take into view the prosperous and happy condition of our country in all the great circumstances which constitute the felicity of a nation—every individual in the full enjoyment of all his rights, the Union blessed with plenty and rapidly rising to greatness under a National Government which operates with complete effect in every part without being felt in any except by the ample protection which it affords, and under State governments which perform their equal share, according to a wise distribution of power between them, in promoting the public happiness—it is impos-

When we view the great blessings with which our country has been favored, those which we now enjoy, and the means which we possess of handing them down unimpaired to our latest posterity, our attention is irresistibly drawn to the source from whence they flow. Let us then, unite in offering our most grateful acknowledgements for these blessings to the Divine Author of All Good.

—SECOND ANNUAL MESSAGE, NOVEMBER 16, 1818

sible to behold so gratifying, so glorious a spectacle without being penetrated with the most profound and grateful acknowledgments to the Supreme Author of All Good for such manifold and inestimable blessings.

—Fourth Annual Message, November 14, 1820

Bliss Isely writes in his *The Presidents: Men of Faith*, that "less is known [about James Monroe's religion] than that of any other President."

Monroe appears not to have discussed or written much at all of religion. His personal correspondence lacks religious references.

David L. Holmes writes of Monroe's faith but provides little fact regarding Monroe's religious belief because little seems to exist. Holmes conjectures that Monroe's silence on religion and his close friendships with Thomas Paine, who after his imprisonment recuperated with the Monroes in Paris for over a year, coupled with the fact that Monroe's alma mater, William and Mary, was a hotbed of deism, all infer that Monroe was at the very least influenced by deism.

Deists don't decide beforehand that God must exist but they come to that conclusion by looking around them and witnessing the order and wonderment of nature.

Einstein understood much of nature and acknowledged what man did not yet know. He believed likely in a deistic type of God. Einstein wrote in 1929: "I believe in Spinoza's God, who reveals himself in the harmony of all that exists, not in a God who concerns himself with the fate and the doings of mankind."

To those who would argue that Monroe or Einstein or anyone drawn to deism is not religious, Einstein writes:

> *The most beautiful emotion we can experience is the mystical. It is the power of all true art and science.*
>
> *He to whom this emotion is a stranger, who can no longer wonder and stand rapt in awe, is as good as dead.*
>
> *To know that what is impenetrable to us really exists, manifesting itself as the highest wisdom and the most radiant beauty, which our dull faculties can*

James Monroe *by Gilbert Sutart c. 1817.*

> *comprehend only in their most primitive forms— this knowledge, this feeling, is at the center of true religiousness.*
>
> *In this sense, and in this sense only, I belong to the rank of devoutly religious men.*

Our founders believed anything was possible. By revolution they had defeated the British Empire. Through science and rational thought some believed that they had discovered a new God that didn't necessarily mean rejection of the old but it did mean that new, scientific thought reinforced their belief in Providence.

I like to think of the founders as discoverers but not as deniers. In some ways Camus was also less denier and more explorer.

Albert Camus was most certainly not a Christian but by all accounts he was not dismissive of those who believed in right and wrong or of Christians in general. In fact, if anything, he wanted Christians to speak out more forcefully against evil in the world. In his essay "The Unbeliever and Christians," Camus writes: "I do not share your (Christian) hope, and I continue to struggle against this universe in which children suffer and die." Struggling to explain evil in the context of an omnipotent God for Camus was a bridge too far.

Yet, Camus was not without hope. In the "Myths of Sisyphus," he imagines Sisyphus descending to renew the thankless and eternal task of rolling the stone up the mountain, but Camus imagines as the rock rolls down the hill and Sisyphus begins his descent that though the task is "sometimes performed in sorrow, it can also take place in joy." I like the way Camus grants Sisyphus the ability to find joy in the relentless return of drudgery. Sisyphus' "fate belongs to him. The rock is his thing." If a man condemned to roll a rock up a hill forever can accept his fate and understand the "rock to be his thing," then there must be hope even for those who lead a normal life filled with much smaller mountains of drudgery.

Camus concludes, "the struggle itself toward the heights is enough to fill a man's heart." One must imagine Sisyphus happy.

Several of the early Presidents have been described as deists, others have used the term theistic rationalists, but whatever the truth, all of them had hope for good to come of rational thought combined with a belief in something greater than man.

6TH

JOHN QUINCY ADAMS

1825-1829

HE HAS CROWNED THE YEAR WITH HIS GOODNESS . . .

The first son of a former president to be elected, Adams began his career as a lawyer and U.S. Senator. He served as Secretary of State under Monroe and continued many of Monroe's policies as president. He pushed for expanded infrastructure in the way of highways and canals, and financed scientific exploration and education. After being defeated by Andrew Jackson in the 1828 election, Monroe was elected to the House of Representatives where he served the rest of his life, notably fighting for civil liberties and opposing slavery.

John Quincy Adams may have been one of the most intelligent, best-educated Presidents in our history. As a teenager, he accompanied his father to Europe. His father let him travel to Russia as the translator for the American ambassador. He spoke half a dozen languages and had visited most of the civilized countries of the world.

He was the most eloquent and vociferous of the Adamses in his opposition to slavery. He was the only President to return to Congress as representative. On foreign policy he preached discretion and advised against the dangers of intervention in foreign war.

As Secretary of State under James Monroe, Adams wrote:

> *"Wherever the standard of freedom and independence has been or shall be unfurled, there will her heart, her benedictions and her prayers be. But [America] goes not abroad in search of monsters to destroy. She is the well-wisher to the freedom and independence of all. She is the champion and vindicator only of*

her own. She will recommend the general cause, by the countenance of her voice, and the benignant sympathy of her example.

She well knows that by once enlisting under other banners than her own, were they even the banners of foreign independence, she would involve herself, beyond the power of extrication, in all the wars of interest and intrigue, of individual avarice, envy, and ambition, which assume the colors and usurp the standard of freedom. The fundamental maxims of her policy would insensibly change from liberty to force.

. . . She might become the dictatress of the world: but she would be no longer the ruler of her own soul . . ."

I particularly admire John Quincy Adams because he talked the talk and he walked the walk. He defended the escaped slaves who took over the Amistad. He fought consistently and valiantly for emancipation and, in his own words, the source of his strength was his faith.

Over the course of the past two years I've been traveling the country and part of this journey has taken me to the inner cities and the churches of the poor. In West Louisville, Rev. Kevin Cosby preaches of faith to a constituency that has little else to rely on. In one of his better-known sermons, Rev. Cosby says, "When you get up in the morning, pray. Before you go to work, pray. When you have to pay a bill, pray. When you need a job, pray. When you need a breakthrough, pray on the Lord, He will. Yes He will."

If the enjoyment in profusion of the bounties of Providence forms a suitable subject of mutual gratulation and grateful acknowledgment, we are admonished at this return of the season when the representatives of the nation are assembled to deliberate upon their concerns to offer up the tribute of fervent and grateful hearts for the never failing mercies of Him who ruleth over all. He has again favored us with healthful seasons and abundant harvests; He has sustained us in peace with foreign countries and in tranquillity within our borders; He has preserved us in the quiet and undisturbed possession of civil and religious liberty; He has crowned the year with His

Southworth & Hawes daguerreotype of John Quincy Adams c. 1850.

goodness, imposing on us no other condition than of improving for our own happiness the blessings bestowed by His hands, and, in the fruition of all His favors, of devoting his faculties with which we have been endowed by Him to His glory and to our own temporal and eternal welfare.

—Fourth Annual Message, December 2, 1828

Why is it, Friends and Fellow Citizens, that you are here assembled . . . ? Why is it that, next to the birthday of the Savior of the World, your most joyous and most venerated festival returns on this day?—And why is it that, among the swarming myriads of our population, thousands and tens of thousands among us, abstaining, under the dictate of religious principle, from the commemoration of that birth-day of Him, who brought life and immortality to light, yet unite with all their brethren of this community, year after year, in celebrating this, the birth-day of the nation?

Is it not that, in the chain of human events, the birthday of the nation is indissolubly linked with the birthday of the Savior? That it forms a leading event in the progress of the gospel dispensation? Is it not that the Declaration of Independence first organized the social compact on the foundation of the Redeemer's mission upon earth? That it laid the corner stone of human government upon the first precepts of Christianity, and gave to the world the first irrevocable pledge of the fulfillment of the prophecies, announced directly from Heaven at the birth of the Savior and predicted by the greatest of the Hebrew prophets six hundred years before?

. . . the Declaration of Independence announced the One People, assuming their station among the powers of the earth, as a civilized, religious, and Christian People, —acknowledging themselves bound by the obligations, and claiming the rights, to which they were entitled by the laws of Nature and of Nature's God . . .

A moral Ruler of the universe, the Governor and Controller of all human power, is the only unlimited sovereign acknowledged by the Declaration of Independence; and it claims for the United States of America, when assuming their equal station among the nations of the earth, only the power to do all that may be done of right

—Independence Day Speech, July 4, 1837

Like John Quincy Adams, I too believe, in metaphor at least, that July 4th and Christmas share many similarities. As Christians, there is no more joyful time of year than Christmas, and being part of a large family makes the celebrations even more fun. Our family is blessed to have many talented singers and guitar players, and we all love to sing carols together with our nephew Matt leading us on guitar. At my parents' house, every dinner starts with a family circle, hands clasped in prayer, and with over forty people, and always at least one new baby, it is a very large circle of love and faith.

Last Christmas we celebrated the wedding of our niece Lisa Paul to Wesley Kimbell. Like her older sister Laura, Lisa is a recent medical school graduate. She plans to follow in the proud tradition of her Aunt Joy and Grandfather Ron as an OB-GYN.

Lisa and Wes are Catholic, and they had their wedding blessed by Pope Francis on a recent trip to Italy. These "sposi novelli" or newlywed blessings are offered on Wednesday afternoons for recent Catholic newlyweds. I'm told it is quite a beautiful and extraordinary sight to see couples filling St. Peter's Square in their wedding attire after receiving papal blessings for their unions. (Lisa wore her mother Peggy's wedding dress since it was easier to transport all the way to Italy.)

During the ceremony, Pope Francis also gave holy blessings over sacred items for the homes of the newlyweds, and Lisa and Wes had an olive wood crucifix blessed as a special gift for Kelley and me. They told us they pray for us as we embark on the endeavor of running for the Presidency of the United States, and they hoped the crucifix would remind us of that.

Kelley and I were so touched by the thoughtfulness and love shown to us by our niece and her husband. It gives me profound encouragement to know that our next generation has people like Lisa and Wes—young men and women of strong faith and conviction. That same Christian faith and conviction gave birth to our great country.

7TH

ANDREW JACKSON

1829 -1837

. . . WITH HEARTS OF THANKFULNESS TO THAT DIVINE BEING WHO HAS FILLED OUR CUP OF PROSPERITY . . .

"Old Hickory" was the state of Tennessee's first member of the House of Representatives. He later served briefly in the Senate. He rose to prominence as a major general in the War of 1812 when he defeated the British at New Orleans. His popularity carried him to the White House, where his contentious personality often clashed with other leaders. Still, Jackson prevailed. His popularity with the American people established his legacy as a man of the common people, as opposed to the privileged aristocrats that dominated government, and his grooming of Vice President Van Buren ensured his policies would continue beyond his years of service.

Jackson presided over the last time in our history we were debt free. Jackson famously fought against government cronyism and disbanded the central bank because he felt its motives were to enrich the monied class at the expense of the common people.

I continue to believe that we've given too much power to our current central bank, the Federal Reserve. With a revolving door between Wall Street, the Treasury, and the Fed, there is a danger that public policy might be tainted by conflicts of interests. Also, I believe Federal Reserve policy, particularly quantitative easing, has eased money into the hands of the wealthy elite who have taken advantage of the stock market boom while much of the rest of America has been left behind, further exacerbating income inequality.

Each year, I'm glad to do dozens of surgeries for people without insurance. I've traveled to Guatemala with a team of talented eye surgeons. There we performed hundreds of cataract surgeries for the poor of that country.

Some might say, well you may like your work but not everyone gets to be an eye surgeon. There is some truth to that but I can honestly say I always got satisfaction from whatever work I did, whether it was the pleasure of the straight lines I mowed as a kid, or the research into the immune status of the eye I did in medical school. It is nearly impossible to describe the joy on the face of a patient who sits up from cataract surgery, smiles, and announces to everyone in the operating room, "I can see again." I love to work, and I know that it's God's will that I work.

"You shall eat the fruit of the labor of your hands; you shall be blessed, and it shall be well with you." —Psalm 128:2

I trust that the God of Isaac and of Jacob will protect you, and give you health in my absence. In Him alone we ought to trust; He alone can preserve and guide us through this troublesome world, and I am sure He will hear your prayers. We are told that the prayers of the righteous prevaileth much, and I add mine for your health and preservation until we meet again.

—Letter to his wife Rachel, December 21, 1823

Andrew Jackson at the Battle of New Orleans January 8, 1814, *mural by Ethel Magafan at the Recorder of Deeds building, Washington, D.C., 1943.*

8TH

MARTIN VAN BUREN

1837–1841

OUR DEVOUT GRATITUDE IS DUE TO THE SUPREME BEING . . .

As an early supporter of Andrew Jackson, the Senator from New York helped Jackson win the White House. Jackson appointed him Secretary of State. After fallout with Vice President John Calhoun, Jackson selected Van Buren as his running mate for his second term.

As president, Van Buren faced the worst depression the young nation had experienced. As an outspoken opponent of slavery, he opposed the annexation of Texas, a move that could also threaten war with Mexico. His popularity waned and his political clout faded with the rise of the Whigs.

> *We have reason to renew the expression of our devout gratitude to the Giver of All Good for His benign protection. Our country presents on every side the evidences of that continued favor under whose auspices it has gradually risen from a few feeble and dependent colonies to a prosperous and powerful confederacy. We are blessed with domestic tranquility and all the elements of national prosperity.*
>
> —FIRST ANNUAL MESSAGE, DECEMBER 5, 1837

Sleepy Hollow Church, Currier & Ives lithograph, 1867.

. . . I only look to the gracious protection of the Divine Being whose strengthening support I humbly solicit, and whom I fervently pray to look down upon us all.

—Martin Van Buren, Inaugural Address, March 4, 1837

9TH

WILLIAM HENRY HARRISON

1841

LET THE NATIONS TO WHOM IT HAS PLEASED GOD TO GIVE ABUNDANCE OF THE COMFORTS OF LIFE, SHARE THEM WITH THEIR NEIGHBORS WHO MAY BE DEFICIENT.

A frontiersman, Harrison fought several campaigns against Indians in the Northwest Territory, which included areas in modern-day Ohio, Indiana, Michigan, Illinois, Wisconsin, and Minnesota. He served as Secretary of the Northwest Territory and its first delegate to Congress. As states formed from the territory, he was elected Governor of Indiana, where he served for 12 years. His military service continued through his governorship, where he won fame at the Battle of Tippecanoe. In the War of 1812, he rose to the rank of brigadier general. After retirement, the Whigs tapped him for president. Though he narrowly won the popular vote, he swept the Electoral College 234 to 60.

In Washington, he relied heavily on Daniel Webster to write his inaugural speech. Unfortunately, its length and the timing proved fatal. After more than two hours in a snowstorm, he caught a cold that developed in pneumonia. He died a month later.

INAUGURAL ADDRESS
March 4, 1841

We admit of no government by divine right, believing that so far as power is concerned the Beneficent Creator has made no distinction amongst men; that all are upon an equality, and that the only legitimate right to govern is an express grant of power from the governed. . . .

These precious privileges, and those scarcely less important of giving expression to his thoughts and opinions, either by writing or speaking, unrestrained but by the liability for injury to others, and that of a full participation in all the advantages which flow from the Government, the acknowledged property of all, the American citizen derives from no charter granted by his fellow-man. He claims them because he is himself a man, fashioned by the same Almighty hand as the rest of his species and entitled to a full share of the blessings with which He has endowed them. . . .

I deem the present occasion sufficiently important and solemn to justify me in expressing to my fellow-citizens a profound reverence for the Christian religion and a thorough conviction that sound morals, religious liberty, and a just sense of religious responsibility are essentially connected with all true and lasting happiness; and to that good Being who has blessed us by the gifts of civil and religious freedom, who watched over and prospered the labors of our fathers and has hitherto preserved to us institutions far exceeding in excellence those of any other people, let us unite in fervently commending every interest of our beloved country in all future time.

Portrait of William Henry Harrison by Rembrandt Peale, c. 1815.

10TH

JOHN TYLER

1841–1845

. . . THE SUPERINTENDENCE OF AN OVERRULING PROVIDENCE HAS BEEN PLAINLY VISIBLE.

The rapid decline and death of President Harrison thrust Vice President John Tyler into the White House. Having served in the House and Senate, as well as governing the state of Virginia, he was respected in the south. However, his differences with the Whigs led to many policy fights and a failed attempt at impeachment. Still, Tyler managed to enact much of his agenda. By the end of his term, he had appointed a cabinet full of supporters of states' rights and slavery. After his presidency, he became a leader in the Democrat party and died in 1862 as a member of the Confederate House of Representatives.

When a Christian people feel themselves to be overtaken by a great public calamity, it becomes them to humble themselves under the dispensation of Divine Providence, to recognize His righteous government over the children of men, to acknowledge His goodness in time past, as well as their own unworthiness, and to supplicate His merciful protection for the future.

The death of William Henry Harrison . . . so soon after his elevation to that high office, is a bereavement peculiarly calculated to be regarded as a heavy affliction, and to impress all minds with a sense of uncertainty of human things, and of the dependence of nations, as well as of individuals, upon our Heavenly Parent.

I have thought, therefore, that I should be acting in conformity with the general expectation and feelings of the community in recommending, as I now do, to the people of the forms of worship, they observe a day of fasting and prayer, by such religious services as may be suitable on the occasion; and I recommend Friday, the fourteenth day of May next, for that purpose; to the end that, on that day, we may all, with one accord, join in humble and reverential approach to Him in whose hands we are, invoking Him to inspire us with a proper spirit and temper of heart and mind under these frowns of His providence, and still to bestow His gracious benedictions upon our government and our country.

—A Recommendation to the People of the United States, April 13, 1841

My earnest prayer shall be constantly addressed to the all-wise and all-powerful Being who made me, and by whose dispensation I am called to the high office of President of this Confederacy, understandingly to carry out the principles of that Constitution which I have sworn "to protect, preserve, and defend."

—Address Upon Assuming the Office of President, April 9, 1841

Wood engraving of Tyler recieving news of Harrison's death.

11TH

JAMES KNOX POLK

1845–1849

AN ALL WISE CREATOR DIRECTED AND GUARDED US IN OUR INFANT STRUGGLE FOR FREEDOM . . .

Polk represented a return to Jacksonian politics, both in domestic and foreign affairs. He worked hard for President Jackson as a member of the House of Representatives, where he served as Speaker between 1835 and 1839. During the Van Buren administration, he left to become Governor of Tennessee. As President, Polk favored westward expansion, working to secure Texas, the Oregon territories, New Mexico, and California. This created new battlegrounds over the issue of slavery, which Polk, a slave owner himself, largely left unaddressed, leaving it to simmer another decade before exploding in war.

I am happy that I can congratulate you on the continued prosperity of our country. Under the blessings of Divine Providence and the benign influence of our free institutions, it stands before the world a spectacle of national happiness. . . .

It becomes us in humility to make our devout acknowledgments to the Supreme Ruler of the Universe for the inestimable civil and religious blessings with which we are favored.

—FIRST ANNUAL MESSAGE, DECEMBER 2, 1845

INAUGURAL ADDRESS
March 4, 1845

In assuming responsibilities so vast I fervently invoke the aid of that Almighty Ruler of the Universe in whose hands are the destinies of nations and of men to guard this Heaven-favored land against the mischiefs which without His guidance might arise from an unwise public policy. With a firm reliance upon the wisdom of Omnipotence to sustain and direct me in the path of duty which I am appointed to pursue, I stand in the presence of this assembled multitude of my countrymen to take upon myself the solemn obligation "to the best of my ability to preserve, protect, and defend the Constitution of the United States."

... Confidently relying upon the aid and assistance of the coordinate departments of the Government in conducting our public affairs, I enter upon the discharge of the high duties which have been assigned me by the people, again humbly supplicating that Divine Being who has watched over and protected our beloved country from its infancy to the present hour to continue His gracious benedictions upon us, that we may continue to be a prosperous and happy people.

Covered Wagons Heading West *by Newell Convers Wyeth*

I wouldn't change anything about my childhood in Lake Jackson, Texas. Okay, perhaps that's overstating it. I had my Holden Caulfield moments. For the most part, though, any discontent took a backseat to baseball cards, Wiffle ball in the backyard and riding my bike everywhere. With fondness, I remember the jobs I held back in those formative years: mowing lawns, working at the Putt-putt golf, and giving swimming lessons. But what I remember most was a feeling of endless time that I would try to fill with daydreams of Walter Mitty magic.

I grew up in the Episcopalian church. My mother taught Sunday school and vacation bible school. I helped with kickball for the vacation bible school (no danger of heresy in a game of kickball). I remember going to church camp on a bus that seemed to break down every other trip, and spending three or four hour stints in a Stuckey's eating those pecan things waiting for the bus to be towed.

Every Sunday we were in church. Well, most of us were. Often, my dad lucked out, or so we thought at the time, and skipped church because he had rounds at the hospital. But my mom and we kids went most every week. I preferred Sunday school to the Sunday service. I won't lie to you. Sometimes I was distracted by the girls in church. Purity of mind can be difficult for a teenager.

Despite my occasional preoccupation, when I was around 15 I knew there was something missing and decided that I would find that in Jesus. It's something that I don't brag about because it didn't always stick. I have a friend who says he has an abiding faith that comes and goes—it was kind of like that for me. Though I wouldn't consider myself a full-fledge Prodigal Son, I did have a tendency to look in places other than my faith for answers.

I read a lot as a teenager. I still love to read. I also loved science from an early age and skepticism is a fundamental part of the study. Doubt propels us to analyze, question and debate. It forces us to go against the tide. Galileo wouldn't have figured out that the world revolves around the sun without doubting common wisdom; Columbus wouldn't have discovered a new world. I was also the son of a doctor and was fascinated by my father's occupation. It was during my sophomore year in high school when I decided I would follow his path. Wearing the arrogant blinders of youth, I saw it as a path filled with deduction and logic and one with little room for God's hand. One of my heroes, Albert Einstein, once said there were only two ways to live your life: "One is as though nothing is a miracle. The other is as though everything is a miracle." In my youth, I believed too much in the former, and too little in the latter. Miracles were for children's stories and after-school specials on TV. I will give myself some credit here though. Once I found my calling, I worked very hard to achieve it. I've always believed that you're doing God's will when you work.

I've also come to find that some of God's best work is done when you're not paying attention.

In church, we used *The Book of Common Prayer*. I recited it ad infinitum and, at the time, the recitation often left me in complete and utter boredom but nevertheless the language sunk in. The exchange with the priest dates back to the third century church and the Anaphora or Apostolic tradition:

Priest: Lift up your hearts.

People: We lift them up unto the LORD.

Priest: Let us give thanks unto the LORD our God.

People: It is meet and right so to do.

The Priest responds: It is very meet, right, and our bounden duty, that we should at all times and in all places, give thanks unto thee, O Lord, Holy Father, Almighty everlasting God.

Now, all these years later, I find myself repeating the liturgy with a depth of conviction that never ceases to amaze me. But I'm getting ahead of myself. Back then I just couldn't wait for church to be over. The benediction below signaled that escape was near: Go forth into the world in peace; be of good courage; hold fast that which is good; render to no man evil for evil; strengthen the fainthearted; support the weak; help the afflicted; honour all men; love and serve the Lord, rejoicing in the power of the Holy Spirit. And the Blessing of God Almighty, the Father, the Son, and the Holy Ghost be upon you, and remain with you forever. Amen.

I don't want you to think that I spent my time rejecting my faith though. I was just a normal teenager who had much more pressing things to think about. As a father now, I can see the same feelings in my own boys. I wish I could just hand my faith to them, but I now know that the path to faith, at least to a lasting faith, is one that must be walked alone.

12TH

ZACHARY TAYLOR

1849–1850

WE SHOULD DO THE BEST WE COULD FOR [OUR FAMILIES], AFTER WHICH TO SUBMIT TO THE DECREES OF AN ALL WISE PROVIDENCE . . .

Despite being a slaveholder residing in Louisiana, Taylor stood firmly on his resolve to preserve the Union. As a general in the Mexican-American War, he rose to popularity as President Polk expanded into Texas and New Mexico. In a three-way race against Democrat Lewis Cass and former president Van Buren, running for the Free Soil Party, Taylor pulled enough votes to win the White House. After only 16 months in office, Taylor suddenly fell ill and died.

We are at peace with all the other nations of the world, and seek to maintain our cherished relations of amity with them. During the past year we have been blessed by a kind Providence with an abundance of the fruits of the earth, and although the destroying angel for a time visited extensive portions of our territory with the ravages of a dreadful pestilence, yet the Almighty has at length deigned to stay his hand and to restore the inestimable blessing of general health to a people who have acknowledged His power, deprecated His wrath, and implored His merciful protection.

—ANNUAL MESSAGE, DECEMBER 4, 1849

INAUGURAL ADDRESS
MARCH 5, 1849

In conclusion I congratulate you, my fellow-citizens, upon the high state of prosperity to which the goodness of Divine Providence has conducted our common country. Let us invoke a continuance of the same protecting care which has led us from small beginnings to the eminence we this day occupy, and let us seek to deserve that continuance by prudence and moderation in our councils, by well-directed attempts to assuage the bitterness which too often marks unavoidable differences of opinion, by the promulgation and practice of just and liberal principles, and by an enlarged patriotism, which shall acknowledge no limits but those of our own widespread Republic.

Southworth & Hawes daguerreotype of Zachary Taylor c. 1850.

13TH

MILLARD FILLMORE

1850–1853

I RELY UPON HIM WHO HOLDS IN HIS HANDS THE DESTINIES OF NATIONS . . .

Taking over for Zachary Taylor, President Fillmore replaced the cabinet with those favoring his policies. To settle several contentious issues, he pushed a compromise that would establish several states' boundaries and allow certain states to maintain slavery. He believed he had averted a national crisis, but instead only delayed it. His signature on the Fugitive Slave Act, which enforced the return of runaway slaves to their owners, irritated those opposed to slavery. Prior to the 1852 elections, he withdrew his name from nomination and ended his years in his hometown of Buffalo, New York.

I cannot bring this communication to a close without invoking you to join me in humble and devout thanks to the Great Ruler of Nations for the multiplied blessings which He has graciously bestowed upon us. His hand, so often visible in our preservation, has stayed the pestilence, saved us from foreign wars and domestic disturbances, and scattered plenty throughout the land. . . . While deeply penetrated with gratitude for the past, let us hope that His all-wise providence will so guide our counsels as that they shall result in giving satisfaction to our constituents, securing the peace of the country, and adding new strength to the united Government under which we live.

—FIRST ANNUAL MESSAGE, DECEMBER 2, 1850

14TH

FRANKLIN PIERCE

1853-1857

I can express no better hope for my country than that the kind Providence which smiled upon our fathers may enable their children to preserve the blessings they have inherited.

Pierce began his career as a lawyer elected to the New Hampshire legislature. He went on to serve in Washington in the House and Senate. In 1852, a supporter proposed his name for president and after a lengthy balloting process, the "dark horse" candidate emerged the winner. He defeated the Whig candidate by a narrow margin to become the fifteenth president. The annulment of the Missouri Compromise during his administration renewed the furor over slavery in new territories, leading to the violence in "bleeding Kansas." At the end of his term, his own party refused to nominate him again, instead favoring James Buchanan.

Although disease, assuming at one time the characteristics of a widespread and devastating pestilence, has left its sad traces upon some portions of our country, we have still the most abundant cause for reverent thankfulness to God for an accumulation of signal mercies showered upon us as a nation. It is well that a consciousness of rapid advancement and increasing strength be habitually associated with an abiding sense of dependence upon Him who holds in His hands the destiny of men and of nations.

—First Annual Message, December 5, 1853

In the present, therefore, as in the past, we find ample grounds for reverent thankfulness to the God of grace and providence for His protecting care and merciful dealings with us as a people. . . . Under the solemnity of these convictions the blessing of Almighty God is earnestly invoked to attend upon your deliberations and upon all the counsels and acts of the Government, to the end that, with common zeal and common efforts, we may, in humble submission to the divine will, cooperate for the promotion of the supreme good of these United States.

—Second Annual Message, December 4, 1854

Portrait of Franklin Pierce, 1853, by George Peter Alexander Healy.

15TH

JAMES BUCHANAN

1857-1861

. . . OUR UNITED PRAYERS OUGHT TO ASCEND TO HIM THAT HE WOULD CONTINUE TO BLESS OUR GREAT REPUBLIC IN TIME TO COME AS HE HAS BLESSED IT IN TIME PAST . . .

Having served in the House and Senate, as well as in the administrations of Polk and Pierce, the Pennsylvanian was viewed as the safe candidate for the Democrats. However, he could not hold a fractious nation together. On the eve of the Civil War, after Republicans had swept the elections and Lincoln became president-elect, Buchanan called for a day of humiliation, fasting, and prayer, but to no avail. Four days later, South Carolina would be the first state to secede.

The Union of the States is at the present moment threatened with alarming and immediate danger; panic and distress of a fearful character prevails throughout the land; our laboring population are without employment, and consequently deprived of the mans of earning their bread. Indeed, hope seems to have deserted the minds of men. All classes are in a state of confusion and dismay, and the wisest counsels of our best and purest men are wholly disregarded.

In this the hour of our calamity and peril, to whom shall we resort for relief but to the God of our fathers? His omnipotent arm only can save us from the awful effects

of our own crimes and follies—our own ingratitude and guilt towards our Heavenly Father.

Let us, then, with deep contrition and penitent sorrow, unite in humbling ourselves before the Most High, in confessing our individual and national sins, and in acknowledging the injustice of our punishment. Let us implore Him to remove from our hearts that false pride of opinion which would impel us to persevere in wrong for the sake of consistency, rather than yield a just submission to the unforeseen exigencies by which we are now surrounded. Let us with deep reverence beseech him to restore the friendship and good will which prevailed in former days among the people of the several States; and, above all, to save us from the horrors of civil war and "blood-guiltiness." Let our fervent prayers ascend to His Throne that He would not desert us in this hour of extreme peril, but remember us as he did our fathers in the darkest days of the revolution; and preserve our Constitution and our Union, the work of their hands, for ages yet to come.

—A Proclamation for Humility, Prayer, and Fasting, December 14, 1860

It is difficult to comprehend the anguish and crushing responsibility of a President dreading the dissolution of the Union under his watch. You feel the weight of this heavy burden in Buchanan's December 14th address.

In "hours of calamity and peril" he turned to prayer, seeking the "omnipotent arm of God" to preserve our union. His fervent prayer reminds me of my journey to Israel two years ago, accompanied by a group of Christian and Jewish leaders.

Kelley and I received Communion at the Garden Tomb in Jerusalem, the site where some believe Jesus was buried and resurrected. The spiritual enormity that this holy place represents dwarfs even mankind's greatest fears and problems.

Inauguration of James Buchanan March 4, 1857.

16TH

ABRAHAM LINCOLN

1861–1865

WITH MALICE TOWARD NONE, WITH CHARITY FOR ALL, WITH FIRMNESS IN THE RIGHT AS GOD GIVES US TO SEE THE RIGHT . . .

Between Lincoln's election and inauguration, seven states seceded. Following through on his vow to preserve the Union, he summoned volunteer troops after Confederate forces took control of Fort Sumter, firing the first shots of the Civil War. President Lincoln would preside over a bloody war that claimed the lives of over half a million Americans. As Union forces moved closer to victory, Lincoln easily won a second term. A month after his second inauguration, on April 9, 1865, Robert E. Lee formally surrendered. Five days later, the president was assassinated.

Lincoln presided over a great internal struggle, a war between brothers, a war between neighbors. The war furrowed his brow. You can visibly see the anguish it caused him, the consternation etched in his features.

I believe that far too many of our leaders fail to properly acknowledge the human agony that always accompanies war. Lincoln was by no means a saint and like all men of his time must bear the responsibility for not discovering a solution short of war, but history judges Lincoln as a contemplative President who despaired over the tragedy that was the Civil War.

Jesus taught us "Blessed are the peacemakers," not Blessed are the warmakers. I don't take this to mean we must be pacifists but I think war and violence of any kind should be reserved for self-defense.

I can recall no utterance of Jesus in favor of war or any acts of aggression. In fact, his message to his disciples was one of non-resistance. I do not believe that means that we don't defend ourselves. I believe individuals and countries can and should defend themselves. But I simply can't imagine Jesus at the head of any army of soldiers and I think as Christians we need to be wary of the doctrine of pre-emptive war.

As we sit here, our brave troops risk their lives, serving our country with faithfulness and honor. They endure harsh conditions, loneliness and great danger. I pray for their safe return each day and I pray for an end to the war.

We must and should stand with our fellow Christians in the Middle East and around the world—but that does not necessarily mean war and it certainly does not mean arming sides in every conflict.

Today, we have a culture that accepts the wanton disposal of millions of innocent children, and sends aid to countries that persecute Christians. I, for one, will not rest until this injustice ends.

As Christians, we understand that the right to life, and freedom of religion, pre-exist all government. These rights are not granted to man by other men, these rights are granted to us by our Creator.

God, help us in these troubling times to make wise decisions, to make moral decisions, and to listen to the voice of God that lives and breathes and resides in us.

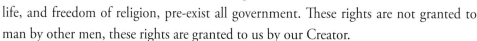

Photo of Abraham Lincoln by Alexander Gardner taken February 5, 1865.

To me, there is no greater responsibility for any legislator or any leader than to determine when we go to war. The consequences are grave and rife with personal tragedy. The war-making responsibility should never be given to any individual who cavalierly calls for war.

War brings with it great obligations.

These obligations do not end when our brave young men and women return home: that is just the beginning. We owe a debt of gratitude to the men and women who fight for our Bill of Rights and no one should ever forget it.

We owe the next generation of warriors the wisdom to know when war is necessary and when war is not the answer.

No one can accuse Lincoln of being cavalier about war.

John Hay, secretary to President Lincoln, found a fragment of writing in Lincoln's desk drawer after his assassination that lays bare the anguish of war that consumed Lincoln.

Hay described it as "not written to be seen of men" and that in it "Mr. Lincoln admits us into the most secret recesses of his soul . . . Perplexed and afflicted beyond the power of human help, by the disasters of war, the wrangling of parties, and the inexorable and constraining logic of his own mind, he shut out the world one day, and tried to put into form his double sense of responsibility to human duty and Divine Power; and this was the result. It shows—as has been said in another place—the awful sincerity of a perfectly honest soul, trying to bring itself into closer communion with its Maker."

The burden of commander in chief is evident in his words. When I think of Lincoln's struggle to discern God's will and purpose, I remember the first time I read *All Quiet on the Western Front* by Erich Maria Remarque. I was fifteen years old, and as I read about the relentless and merciless charges from one trench to another, the utter carnage, I wondered, whose grand design was this?

Shortly afterward, I read *Silent Night: The Story of the World War I Christmas Truce* by Stanley Weintraub, the story of the Christmas Eve armistice, and I was deeply moved by soldiers that laid down their arms to sing Christmas carols with the enemy, who came out of their trenches to play soccer and exchange small gifts. For one night, they felt God's grace, and through it acknowledged their shared fragile humanity, and understood goodness so profound that it overcame hatred and war.

JUSTICE

Lincoln's attitude toward justice still resonates today: "I have always found that mercy bears richer fruits than strict justice."

For most of us, our religion believes in redemption, in second chances.

Justice is a balance between punishment and rehabilitation. Certainly, justice includes locking up and separating from society violent offenders to keep us all safe.

But there are certainly others who are not beyond a second chance.

Ultimately, justice is found in discernment.

Kalief Browder, a young, black teenager from the Bronx, was imprisoned on Riker's Island for three years and kept there without trial and for much of the time in solitary confinement. This young man's despair caused him to attempt suicide more than once both in jail and on his release. He was finally released without ever going to trial. The illegal immigrant who accused him of a crime fled the country. This past June, Kalief hung himself at his parents' home. When you read Kalief's tragic story, you can begin to understand the discontent afoot in our cities.

Compounding the discontent are the murders of three NYC police officers. The police risk their lives every day and those of us not on the streets cannot fathom the danger they face each day.

Justice will come when we decide that we cannot incarcerate our way to a solution. Questions of justice are not new or unique. Lincoln faced momentous questions hardly fathomable by our generation.

In Lincoln's day, it was the great and long awaited question of emancipation. Today, it is still the struggle for equal protection under the law.

Justice will not be served until systemic racial disparities in the application of justice are eliminated.

In search of justice, in search of an end to conflict, in search of solace in a time of great carnage, Lincoln's eyes drifted heavenward.

Lincoln accepted and understood that actions here on earth would be divinely judged and that as a nation and as a people we would be judged by where we stood in the struggle to end human bondage.

The Peacemakers, *1868 by George Peter Alexander Healy.*

The will of God prevails. In great contests each party claims to act in accordance with the will of God. Both may be, and one must be, wrong. God cannot be for and against the same thing at the same time. In the present civil war it is quite possible that God's purpose is something different from the purpose of either party—and yet the human instrumentalities, working just as they do, are of the best adaptation to effect His purpose. I am almost ready to say that this is probably true—that God wills this contest, and wills that it shall not end yet. By his mere great power, on the minds of the now contestants, He could have either saved or destroyed the Union without a human contest. Yet the contest began. And, having begun He could give the final victory to either side any day. Yet the contest proceeds.

—Abraham Lincoln, *Meditation on the Divine Will*,
Washington, D.C., September, 1862

I know there is a God, and that He hates the injustice of slavery. I see the storm coming, and I know that His hand is in it. If He has a place and a work for me, and I think He has, I believe I am ready. I am nothing, but truth is everything. I know I am right, because I know that liberty is right, for Christ teaches it, and Christ is God.

—Springfield, Illinois 1860

Whereas it is the duty of nations as well as of men to own their dependence upon the overruling power of God, to confess their sins and transgressions in humble sorrow, yet with assured hope that genuine repentance will lead to mercy and pardon, and to recognize the sublime truth, announced in the Holy Scriptures and proven by all history, that those nations only are blessed whose God is the Lord;

And, insomuch as we know that by His divine law nations, like individuals, are subjected to punishments and chastisements in this world, may we not justly fear that the awful calamity of civil war which now desolates the land may be but a punishment inflicted upon us for our presumptuous sins, to the needful end of our national reformation as a whole people? We have been the recipients of the choicest bounties of Heaven; we have been preserved these many years in peace and prosperity; we have grown in numbers, wealth, and power as no other nation has ever grown. But we have forgotten God. We have forgotten the gracious hand which preserved us in peace and multiplied and enriched and strengthened us, and we have vainly imagined, in the deceitfulness of our hearts, that all these blessings were produced by some superior wisdom and virtue of our own. Intoxicated with unbroken success, we have become too self-sufficient to feel the necessity of redeeming and preserving grace, too proud to pray to the God that made us.

It behooves us, then, to humble ourselves before the offended Power, to confess our national sins, and to pray for clemency and forgiveness.

—A Proclamation by the President, March 30, 1863

Lincoln The Rail Spliter, *print c. 1909 after a painting by J.L.G. Ferris.*

17TH

ANDREW JOHNSON

1865–1869

AN ALL-WISE AND MERCIFUL PROVIDENCE HAS ABATED THE PESTILENCE WHICH VISITED OUR SHORES . . .

As a Southern Democrat, Johnson had a keen interest in reconstruction after the war. His moves irritated many Northerners, but he managed to restore a significant level of peace in the ravaged nation. When he vetoed the Civil Rights Act of 1866, which established freed blacks as American citizens and forbade discrimination against them, the Congress over-rode his veto. A few months later Congress proposed the Fourteenth Amendment, which stipulated that no state should "deprive any person of life, liberty, or property, without due process of law."

Johnson would continue to clash with Congress. He escaped impeachment by just one vote. In the 1868 election, his party abandoned him and put forth Horatio Seymour, the former governor of New York. He lost by a wide margin of electoral votes to the Civil War hero, General Ulysses S. Grant.

To express gratitude to God in the name of the people for the preservation of the United States is my first duty in addressing you. . . .

The Union of the United States of America was intended by its authors to last as long as the States themselves shall last. "The Union shall be perpetual" are the words of the Confederation. "To form a more perfect Union," by an ordinance of the people of the United States, is the declared purpose of the Constitution. The hand of Divine Providence was never more plainly visible in the affairs of men than in the framing and the adopting of that instrument. . . .

Where in past history does a parallel exist to the public happiness which is within the reach of the people of the United States? Where in any part of the globe can institutions be found so suited to their habits or so entitled to their love as their own free Constitution? Every one of them, then, in whatever part of the land he has his home, must wish its perpetuity. Who of them will not now acknowledge, in the words of Washington, that "every step by which the people of the United States have advanced to the character of an independent nation seems to have been distinguished by some token of providential agency"? Who will not join with me in the prayer that the Invisible Hand which has led us through the clouds that gloomed around our path will so guide us onward to a perfect restoration of fraternal affection that we of this day may be able to transmit our great inheritance of State governments in all their rights, of the General Government in its whole constitutional vigor, to our posterity, and they to theirs through countless generations?

—First Annual Message, December 4, 1865

Let us earnestly hope that before the expiration of our respective terms of service, now rapidly drawing to a close, an all-wise Providence will so guide our counsels as to strengthen and preserve the Federal Unions, inspire reverence for the Constitution, restore prosperity and happiness to our whole people, and promote "on earth peace, good will toward men."

—Fourth Annual Message, December 9, 1868

Illustration of Andrew Jackson's impeachment from the April 11, 1868 issue of Harper's Weekly.

18TH

ULYSSES S. GRANT

1869 ~ 1877

. . . IT IS WITH GRATITUDE TO THE GIVER OF ALL GOOD FOR THE MANY BENEFITS WE ENJOY.

Having been promoted to General-in-Chief by President Lincoln and presiding over the surrender of Robert E. Lee, officially ending the war, the military hero easily captured the White House. Being a military man, not a politician, the machinations of Washington caused him much difficulty. Still, he maintained the policies of reconstruction put forth by the Radicals, furthered the cause of African-Americans, and held the peace for two terms.

The year which is drawing to a close has been free from pestilence–health has prevailed throughout the land—abundant crops reward the labors of Husbandman—commerce and manufacturers have successfully prosecuted their peaceful paths—the mines and forest have yielded liberally—the Nation has increased in wealth and in strength—peace has prevailed; and its blessings have advanced every interest of the People, in every part of the Union. Harmony and fraternal intercourse restored, are obliterating the marks of past conflict and estrangement. Burdens have been lightened—means have been increased—civil and religious liberty are secured to every inhabitant of the land, whose soil is trod by none but freemen.

It becomes a people thus favored to make acknowledgement to the Supreme Author from whom such blessings flow, of their gratitude and their dependence—to render praise and thanksgiving for the same, and devoutly to implore a continuance of God's mercies.

Therefore, I, Ulysses S. Grant, President of the United States, do recommend that Thursday the 18th day of November next, be observed as a day of Thanksgiving and of Praise and of Prayer to Almighty God, the Creator and Ruler of the Universe. And I do further recommend to all the people of the United States to assemble on that day in their accustomed places of public worship and to unite in the homage and praise due to the Bountiful Father of all mercies and in fervent prayer for the continuance of the manifold blessings he has vouchsafed to us as a People:

In testimony whereof, I have hereunto set my hand and caused the Seal of the United States to be affixed, this fifth day of October, A.D. eighteen hundred and sixty nine, and of the Independence of the United States of America the Ninety fourth.

—Thanksgiving Proclamation, October 5, 1869

I have always looked forward to Thanksgiving—the tang of Autumn, the gathering of family newly embarked on a fresh school year, the jostle and steam in the kitchen as many hands season dishes with loving care. It is perhaps my favorite holiday. I love that as a nation we have set aside an entire day to simply acknowledge our gratitude to our Creator for all the goodness of life, for the blessings of being part of a country that has been endowed with not only incredible natural resources and beauty, but a legacy of courage, faith and freedom.

At Thanksgiving we express thanks for our national heritage, but also for love, family, and friendship, the most precious gifts of all. At our house, in addition to the preparation of the traditional feast, our family gathers with cousins, aunts and uncles, and friends for touch football in our backyard.

I make the turkey each year, an all-day labor of love involving fresh herbs chopped and layered beneath the skin and a baste of madeira wine and butter. The food is glorious, of course, but it also feeds the soul. As we gather in a circle of clasped hands and bowed heads, young and old, for the prayer, I always feel a surge of tender emotion and gratitude for the blessings of my home and family.

19TH

RUTHERFORD B. HAYES

1877–1881

BY THE FAVOR OF DIVINE PROVIDENCE
WE HAVE BEEN BLESSED . . .

After serving in the House right after the Civil War, then three terms as the Governor of Ohio, Republicans tapped Hayes at the end of Grant's second term. In a highly contested election, he lost the popular vote but was deemed the winner by an electoral tally of 185-184. In office, he began withdrawing troops from the South, hoping to erase the lines between North and South. He also reformed the Indian Bureau and attempted to assimilate tribes in the American culture. At the end of his term, he kept his promise to retire and spent the rest of his life promoting education and prison reform.

Under a sense of these infinite obligations to the Great Ruler of Times and Seasons and Events, let us humbly ascribe it to our own faults and frailties if in any degree that perfect concord and happiness, peace and justice, which such great mercies should diffuse through the hearts and lives of our people do not altogether and always and everywhere prevail. Let us with one spirit and with one voice lift up praise and thanksgiving to God for His manifold goodness to our land, His manifest care for our nation.

—THANKSGIVING PROCLAMATION, OCTOBER 29, 1877

Rutherford B. Hayes by Mathew Brady, c. 1880.

Our heartfelt gratitude is due to the Divine Being who holds in His hands the destinies of nations for the continued bestowal during the last year of countless blessings upon our country.

—Second Annual Message, December 2, 1878

20TH

JAMES A. GARFIELD

1881

I NEED MORE FAITH. FAITH COMES BY HEARING, AND HEARING BY THE WORD OF GOD.

Garfield is sometimes referred to as "the preacher president," since he preached until he was elected to congress, although not as an ordained minister. He had become a Christian at a Disciples of Christ Church camp meeting in 1850, where he was baptized. He chronicled the experience by writing; "Today I was buried with Christ in baptism and arose to walk in the newness of life."

After rising to the rank of Major General during the war, Garfield was elected to the House in 1862, where he served for 18 years. He was nominated by Republicans in 1880 and defeated the Democrat by only 10,000 votes. Garfield resigned as an elder in his church when he was elected President, stating emphatically, "I resign the highest office in the land to become President of the United States."

Less than four months into President Garfield's term, he was shot by a disillusioned and deranged supporter, Charles J. Guiteau. He died eleven weeks later on September 19.

It is clear to my mind, that the theological and formal part of Christianity has in great measure lost its power over the minds of men. But the life and Christianity of Christ are to me as precious and perfect as ever.

—THE DIARY OF JAMES GARFIELD, NOVEMBER 23, 1873

FIRST INAUGURAL ADDRESS
March 4, 1881

I shall greatly rely upon the wisdom and patriotism of Congress and of those who may share with me the responsibilities and duties of administration, and, above all, upon our efforts to promote the welfare of this great people and their Government I reverently invoke the support and blessings of Almighty God.

If elected, it will be my purpose to enforce strict obedience to the constitution and the laws, and to promote, as best I may, the interest and honor of the whole country, relying for support upon the wisdom of Congress, the intelligence and patriotism of the people and the favor of God.

—Letter Accepting the Presidential Nomination, July 12, 1880

The arrest of James Garfield's assassin from the July 16, 1881 issue of Frank Leslie's Illustrated Newspaper.

21ST

CHESTER A. ARTHUR

1881-1885

...WE OWE TO THE GIVER OF ALL GOOD
OUR REVERENT ACKNOWLEDGMENT.

The son of a Baptist minister, Arthur sought to rise above the political fray of his time, often avoiding political acquaintances in public. His reforms aimed at restricting political corruption and his reduction in tariffs attempted to trim bloated government coffers. Despite being thrust into office by the assassination of the president, Arthur gained the respect of the country and many of his peers. Unknown to the public at the time, he was suffering from a fatal kidney disease while in office. At the end of his term, he kept his name in the running, but was not nominated again. He died two years later.

It has long been the pious custom of our people, with the closing of the year, to look back upon the blessings brought to them in the changing course of the seasons and to return solemn thanks to the all-giving source from whom they flow. And although at this period, when the falling leaf admonishes us that the time of our sacred duty is at hand, our nation still lies in the shadow of a great bereavement, and the mourning which has filled our hearts still finds its sorrowful expression toward the God before whom we but lately bowed in grief and supplication, yet the countless benefits which have showered upon us during the past twelvemonth call for our fervent gratitude and make it fitting that we should rejoice with thankfulness that the Lord in His

infinite mercy has most signally favored our country and our people. Peace without and prosperity within have been vouchsafed to us, no pestilence has visited our shores, the abundant privileges of freedom which our fathers left us in their wisdom are still our increasing heritage; and if in parts of our vast domain sore affliction has visited our brethren in their forest homes, yet even this calamity has been tempered and in a manner sanctified by the generous compassion for the sufferers which has been called forth throughout our land. For all these things it is meet that the voice of the nation should go up to God in devout homage.

—Thanksgiving Proclamation, November 4, 1881

Portrait of Chester A. Arthur, 1881 by Ole Peter Hansen Balling.

FIRST INAUGURAL ADDRESS
MARCH 4, 1885

And let us not trust to human effort alone, but humbly acknowledging the power and goodness of Almighty God, who presides over the destiny of nations, and who has at all times been revealed in our country's history, let us invoke His aid and His blessings upon our labors.

22ND & 24TH

GROVER CLEVELAND

1885-1889, 1893-1897

THE PEOPLE OF THE UNITED STATES SHOULD NEVER BE UNMINDFUL OF THE GRATITUDE THEY OWE THE GOD OF NATIONS FOR HIS WATCHFUL CARE . . .

The only president to win two non-successive terms, Cleveland was the first Democrat to win the White House since the Civil War. The son of a Presbyterian minister, he rose quickly into politics first as the Mayor of Buffalo, then the Governor of New York. Early in his first term, Cleveland married Frances Folsom, who, at 21, was less than half his age. He narrowly lost his second election to the Republican, but returned four years later to defeat him. Both terms were marked by fiscal conservatism and attempts to thwart corruption.

In accepting his party's nomination, Cleveland wrote that he would depend "upon the favor and support of the Supreme Being Who, I believe, will always bless honest human endeavor in the conscientious discharge of public duty."

His daughter Ruth's death in 1904 caused an anguished Cleveland to question God's existence: "I had a season of great trouble in keeping out of my mind the ideas that Ruth was in the cold cheerless grave instead of in the arms of her Savior." But he would later write in his diary that his faith gave him some measure of comfort, "God has come to my help and I am able to adjust my thought to dear Ruth's death with as much comfort as selfish humanity will permit."

Portrait of Grover Cleveland, 1889 by Anders Zorn.

One of my favorite quotes of Cleveland's is "What is the use of being elected or reelected, unless you stand for something?" I remind myself of that quote often in Washington as I see all around me people who have chosen to get elected but without choosing to stand for anything.

I believe life is sacred from the moment of conception to our last natural breath. There is no greater of God's gifts to us. Can a country, founded on God-given rights, continue to thrive without understanding that life is precious, a gift from our Creator? I think not. Since the *Roe v. Wade* decision, over 50 million innocent children have been killed in abortion procedures. As a physician I find this unconscionable. Under the 14th Amendment, it is the government's duty to protect life as defined in our Constitution. As a United States Senator, and a man of faith, it is my duty to fight for that right. I believe there will come a time when we will all be judged for the stand we take in defense of life.

Our mission among the nations of the earth and our success in accomplishing the work God has given the American people to do require of those intrusted with the making and execution of our laws perfect devotion, above all other things, to the public good.

—Fourth Annual Message, December 3, 1888

SECOND INAUGURAL ADDRESS
March 4, 1893

It cannot be doubted that our stupendous achievements as a people and our country's robust strength have given rise to heedlessness of those laws governing our national health which we can no more evade than human life can escape the laws of God and nature....

Above all, I know there is a Supreme Being who rules the affairs of men and whose goodness and mercy have always followed the American people, and I know He will not turn from us now if we humbly and reverently seek His powerful aid.

23RD

BENJAMIN HARRISON

1889-1893

. . . GRATITUDE AND PRAISE TO OUR BENEFICENT CREATOR FOR THE RICH BLESSINGS HE HAS GRANTED TO US AS A NATION . . .

The grandson of William Henry Harrison began as a lawyer in Ohio, served as a Colonel in the Civil War, and won a senatorial seat in the 1880s. During his years as a soldier in the Civil War, Harrison was known for holding prayer meetings in his tent each night. During that time he wrote a letter to his wife asking her to pray "first that He will enable me to bear myself as a good soldier of Jesus Christ; second that He will give me valor and skill to conduct myself so as to honor my country and my friends."

In another letter to a friend, Harrison wrote, "It is a great comfort to trust God—even if His providence is unfavorable. Prayer steadies one when he is walking in slippery places—even if things asked for are not given."

Although he lost the popular vote to the incumbent president, he carried a sizeable margin of electoral votes to claim the White House. He vigorously advocated an amenable foreign policy, expanded the navy, and signed the Sherman Anti-Trust Act to bust the monopolies. His high spending and the vehement opposition to his high taxes drained the Treasury surplus and cost him a second term.

FIRST INAUGURAL ADDRESS
MARCH 4, 1889

Entering thus solemnly into covenant with each other, we may reverently invoke and confidently expect the favor and help of Almighty God—that He will give to me wisdom, strength, and fidelity, and to our people a spirit of fraternity and a love of righteousness and peace. . . .

No other people have a government more worthy of their respect and love or a land so magnificent in extent, so pleasant to look upon, and so full of generous suggestion to enterprise and labor. God has placed upon our head a diadem and has laid at our feet power and wealth beyond definition or calculation. But we must not forget that we take these gifts upon the condition that justice and mercy shall hold the reins of power and that the upward avenues of hope shall be free to all the people.

A highly favored people, mindful of their dependence on the bounty of Divine Providence, should seek fitting occasion to testify gratitude and ascribe praise to Him who is the author of their many blessings. It behooves us, then, to look back with thankful hearts over the past year and bless God for His infinite mercy in vouchsafing to our land enduring peace, to our people freedom from pestilence and famine, to our husbandmen abundant harvests, and to them that labor a recompense of their toil.

—THANKSGIVING PROCLAMATION, NOVEMBER 1, 1889

Now, therefore, I, Benjamin Harrison, President of the United States of America, in response to this pious and reasonable request, do recommend that on Tuesday, April 30, at the hour of 9 o'clock in the morning, the people of the entire country repair to their respective places of divine worship to implore the favor of God that the blessings of liberty, prosperity, and peace may abide with us as a people, and that His hand may lead us in the paths of righteousness and good deeds.

—WASHINGTON CENTENNIAL ANNIVERSARY, APRIL 4, 1889

25TH

WILLIAM MCKINLEY

1897–1901

OUR EARNEST PRAYER IS THAT GOD WILL GRACIOUSLY VOUCHSAFE PROSPERITY AND HAPPINESS AND PEACE TO ALL OUR NEIGHBORS AND LIKE BLESSINGS TO ALL THE PEOPLES AND POWERS OF THE EARTH.

McKinley was an Ohio lawyer and Civil War veteran elected to Congress. After fourteen years in the House, he won the Governor's office in Ohio twice before running for president. Early in his first term, he presided over the Spanish-American War, which lasted little more than three months and led to the annexation of the Philippines, Puerto Rico, and Guam. Of his decision to intervene in the Philippines, McKinley said to a General Missionary Committee of the Methodist Episcopal Church: "I walked the floor of the White House night after night until midnight, and I am not ashamed to tell you gentlemen, that I went down on my knees and prayed to Almighty God for light and guidance more than one night."

Seven months into his second term, he was shot by anarchist Leon Czolgosz. McKinley died eight days later on September 14, 1901, but not before publicly forgiving his assassin.

When I think of the generosity of spirit that such forgiveness demands, I seek to remember that Jesus is our example in forgiving those who "trespass against us."

FIRST INAUGURAL ADDRESS
March 4, 1897

In obedience to the will of the people, and in their presence, by the authority vested in me by this oath, I assume the arduous and responsible duties of President of the United States, relying upon the support of my countrymen and invoking the guidance of Almighty God. Our faith teaches that there is no safer reliance than upon the God of our fathers, who has so singularly favored the American people in every national trial, and who will not forsake us so long as we obey His commandments and walk humbly in His footsteps.

"When they came to the place that is called The Skull, they crucified him there with the criminals, one on the right and the other on the left. Jesus said, "Father, forgive them, for they don't know what they are doing." —Luke 23:33-34

The bad thief, as the story goes, said to Jesus on the cross, "Are you not the Christ? Save yourself and us!" On the other side of Jesus hung Dismas, the good thief. "We are receiving the due reward of our deeds," he said, "but this man has done nothing wrong." He then turned his head to the Lord, "Jesus, remember me when you come into your kingdom," he said. And then came one of the great promises of the New Testament. "Truly," Jesus said, "today you will be with me in paradise."

I am a Christian and I believe in second chances. This is why I feel so passionately about the Redeem Act, legislation I've proposed with Senator Cory Booker that will allow those in our community who deserve a second chance to have one by removing the shackles of a permanent criminal record.

I therefore ask the people of the United States, upon next assembling for divine worship in their respective places of meeting, to offer thanksgiving to Almighty God, who in His inscrutable ways, now leading our hosts upon the waters to unscathed triumph, now guiding them in a strange land, through the dread shadows of death, to success, even though at a fearful cost; now bearing them, without accident or loss, to far distant climes, has watched over our cause and brought nearer the success of the right and the attainment of just and honorable peace. . . .

And above all, let us pray with earnest fervor that He, the Dispense of All Good, may speedily remove from us the untold afflictions of war and bring to our dear land the blessings of restored peace and to all the domain now ravaged by the cruel strife the priceless boon of security and tranquility.

—Executive Proclamation, July 6, 1898

Never has this Nation had more abundant cause than during the past year for thankfulness to God for manifold blessings and mercies, for which we make reverent acknowledgment.

—Third Annual Message, December 5, 1899

Edwin Everett Hale was the chaplain of the Senate at the turn of the twentieth century. He was asked by a visitor to the Capitol, "Do you pray for the Senators?" He replied, "I look at the Senators and I pray for the country."

The current Senate Chaplain would likely understand the humor.

Each day, Congress is opened by a prayer given by the Senate Chaplain, Barry C. Black. Chaplain Black is a retired Rear Admiral who served in the U.S. Navy for more than 27 years, where he also served as Chief of Navy Chaplains.

Chaplain Black's prayers, given in his distinctive deep baritone, never fail to inspire me, and I am deeply grateful for the prayers he also lifts up for every senator by name each day.

Chaplain Black, who grew up in poverty with an alcoholic father, overcame daunting challenges to become a man who has given inspiration and courage to thousands through his distinguished careers as a military officer, chaplain and author.

In his book *The Blessing of Adversity: Finding Your God Given Purpose in Life's Troubles*, Chaplain Black writes about using our pain and struggles as a way to discern God's purpose in our lives. He prays for wisdom for those of us in positions of leadership. I am reminded of this verse: "Yes, if you call out for insight and raise your voice for understanding, if you seek it like silver and search for it as for hidden treasures, then you will understand the fear of the Lord and find the knowledge of God." —Proverbs 2:3-5

26TH

THEODORE ROOSEVELT

1901–1909

AGAINST THE WRATH OF THE LORD
THE WISDOM OF MAN CANNOT AVAIL.

With McKinley's assassination, 42-year-old Teddy Roosevelt became the youngest president in our nation's history. He was a hero of the Spanish-American War, serving as lieutenant colonel of the famed Rough Rider Regiment and leading the charge at the battle of San Juan. His mantra of "speak softly and carry a big stick" carried him through anti-trust battles with railroads and other big businesses. He presided over the initiation of the Panama Canal and mediated the end of the Russo-Japanese war. His love of the outdoors led him to set aside massive amounts of public lands in the West. When he left office after his second term, he went on an African safari.

In the midst of our affliction we reverently thank the Almighty that we are at peace with the nations of mankind; and we firmly intend that our policy shall be such as to continue unbroken these international relations of mutual respect and good will.

—FIRST ANNUAL MESSAGE, DECEMBER 3, 1901

Kurz & Allison print of Col. Theodore Roosevelt and the Rough Riders.

SECOND INAUGURAL ADDRESS
March 4, 1905

My fellow-citizens, no people on earth have more cause to be thankful than ours, and this is said reverently, in no spirit of boastfulness in our own strength, but with gratitude to the Giver of Good who has blessed us with the conditions which have enabled us to achieve so large a measure of well-being and of happiness.

Every thinking man, when he thinks, realizes what a very large number of people tend to forget, that the teachings of the Bible are so interwoven and entwined with our whole civic and social life that it would be literally—I do not mean figuratively, I mean literally—impossible for us to figure ourselves what that life would be if these teachings were removed. We would lose almost all the standards by which we now judge both public and private morals; all the standards which we, with more or less resolution, strive to raise ourselves. Almost every man who has by his life work added to the sum of human achievement of which the race is proud, of which our people are proud, almost every such man has based his life work largely upon the teachings of the Bible.

—Long Island Bible Society, 1901

While I'm not a great fan of Teddy Roosevelt, his "man in the arena" speech quoted below is one of the best exhortations to take action and get involved in the political process.

"It is not the critic who counts; not the man who points out how the strong man stumbles, or where the doer of deeds could have done them better. The credit belongs to the man who is actually in the arena, whose face is marred by dust and sweat and blood; who strives valiantly; who errs, who comes short again and again, because there is no effort without error and shortcoming; but who does actually strive to do the deeds; who knows great enthusiasms, the great devotions; who spends himself in a worthy cause; who at the best knows in the end the triumph of high achievement, and who at the worst, if he fails, at least fails while daring greatly, so that his place shall never be with those cold and timid souls who neither know victory nor defeat."

Perhaps there is no other arena where the lights shine as brightly as running for president, and no other stage where one's vulnerability is more on display. Dr. Brené Brown, professor at the University of Houston Graduate College of Social Work, tells us that vulnerability is not a weakness, but rather "our most accurate measurement of courage." I agree, but I also believe that courage doesn't come from internal fortitude. It is a gift from God. God grants us the courage to be vulnerable, to rise up again after we fall, to stand for what we believe. It is not one's own strength that supplies the daring to survive the arena in this fashion, and anyone who thinks it is doesn't deserve to be there in the first place. This strength comes from a faith in God. Without it we are but a noisy gong, a clanging symbol, an empty suit.

ABOVE: Theodore Roosevelt, 1910.
FOLLOWING PAGES: The Grand Canyon of the Yellowstone, *1893–1901 by Thomas Moran.*

The things of the body are good; the things of the intellect better; the best of all are the things of the soul; for, in the nation as in the individual, in the long run it is character that counts.

27TH

WILLIAM HOWARD TAFT

1909–1913

IT IS ALTOGETHER FITTING THAT WE SHOULD HUMBLY AND GRATEFULLY ACKNOWLEDGE THE DIVINE SOURCE OF THESE BLESSINGS.

Handpicked by President Roosevelt to succeed him, Taft served as Secretary of War under his predecessor. However, his purposeful adherence to the law limited him from being as aggressive in his ambitions and his departures from some of Roosevelt's policies irritated his party. He did preside over the push to have states amend their constitutions to allow a federal income tax and he eliminated Senatorial appointments, turning it into a popular vote. As his term expired, Republicans re-nominated him, but Teddy Roosevelt returned to the scene as the Progressive Party candidate, splitting the vote and handing victory to the Democrat.

Harris & Ewing photograph of William Howard Taft, 1905.

FIRST INAUGURAL ADDRESS
March 4, 1909

I invoke the considerate sympathy and support of my fellow-citizens and the aid of the Almighty God in the discharge of my responsible duties.

I have no doubt that when these young ladies grow to womanhood they will have the ballot, but whether you do or not you ought to make preparation to understand your country and to know the gratitude you ought to offer to God for being Americans.

—Campaign in Woodbury, Delaware, May 28, 1912

Our country has been signally favored in many ways. The round of the seasons has brought rich harvests. Our industries have thrived far beyond our domestic needs; the productions of our labor are daily finding enlarged markets abroad. We have been free from the curses of pestilence, of famine and of war. Our national councils have furthered the cause of peace in other lands, and the spirit of benevolence has brought us into closer touch with other peoples, to the strengthening of the bonds of fellowship and good will that link us to our comrades in the universal brotherhood of nations. Strong in the sense of our own rights and inspired by as strong a sense of the rights of others, we live in peace and harmony with the world. Rich in the priceless possessions and abundant resources wherewith the unstinted bounty of God has endowed us, we are unselfishly glad when other peoples pass onward to prosperity and peace. That the great privileges we enjoy may continue and that each coming year may see our country more firmly established in the regard and esteem of our fellow nations is the prayer that should arise in every thankful heart.

—Thanksgiving Proclamation, October 30, 1911

28TH

WOODROW WILSON

1913–1921

THE YEAR THAT HAS JUST PASSED HAS BEEN MARKED IN A PECULIAR DEGREE BY MANIFESTATIONS OF HIS GRACIOUS AND BENEFICENT PROVIDENCE.

Wilson was raised in the deep South during the Civil War. His father, a Presbyterian minister, pastored a church in Augusta, Georgia, during the war and Wilson was a professor in the ravaged city of Columbia, South Carolina, during Reconstruction. In 1902, he returned to his alma mater to serve as the president of Princeton. Democrats persuaded him to run for office, leading him to become Governor of New Jersey in 1910. Two years later, he won only 42 percent of the popular vote, but easily carried the electoral college in the three-way race.

Once in office, Wilson implemented a graduated federal income tax, established the Federal Trade Commission, and passed a massive amount of varied legislation just prior to his reelection bid. Despite campaigning with the slogan "he kept us out of war," he realized war was inevitable and on April 12, 1917, asked Congress to authorize the United States' entry into World War I.

There are times when words seem empty and only actions seem great. Such a time has come, and in the providence of God, America will once more have an opportunity to show the world that she was born to serve mankind.

—MEMORIAL DAY SPEECH, MAY 30, 1917

FIRST INAUGURAL ADDRESS
March 5, 1913

The feelings with which we face this new age of right and opportunity sweep across our heartstrings like some air out of God's own presence, where justice and mercy are reconciled and the judge and the brother are one.

And while we render thanks for these things let us pray Almighty God that in all humbleness of spirit we may look always to Him for guidance; that we may be kept constant in the spirit and purpose of service; that by His grace our minds may be directed and our hands strengthened; and that in His good time liberty and security and peace and the comradeship of a common justice may be vouchsafed all the nations of the earth.

—Thanksgiving Proclamation, November 7, 1917

Woodrow Wilson's inauguration March 5, 1917.

29TH

WARREN G. HARDING

1921–1923

I MUST UTTER MY BELIEF IN THE DIVINE INSPIRATION OF THE FOUNDING FATHERS. SURELY THERE MUST HAVE BEEN GOD'S INTENT IN THE MAKING OF THIS NEW-WORLD REPUBLIC. . . .

The Ohio newspaper publisher began his political career by serving in the state Senate and as Lieutenant Governor before being elected to the U.S. Senate in 1914. Six years later, he emerged as the Republican nominee and ran on a campaign of "less government in business and more business in government." He won by a landslide. Halfway through his term, he learned of some scandals within his own administration. He turned to his trusted, honest Secretary of State, Herbert Hoover, for advice. Hoover recommended he go public with the information. However, Harding never had the chance. While traveling out west, he suffered a heart attack in San Francisco and died.

President Warren G. Harding's first cabinet meeting, 1921.

INAUGURAL ADDRESS
MARCH 4, 1921

One cannot stand in this presence and be unmindful of the tremendous responsibility. The world upheaval has added heavily to our tasks. But with the realization comes the surge of high resolve, and there is reassurance in belief in the God-given destiny of our Republic. If I felt that there is to be sole responsibility in the Executive for the America of tomorrow I should shrink from the burden. But here are a hundred millions, with common concern and shared responsibility, answerable to God and country. The Republic summons them to their duty, and I invite co-operation.

I accept my part with single-mindedness of purpose and humility of spirit, and implore the favor and guidance of God in His Heaven. With these I am unafraid, and confidently face the future.

I have taken the solemn oath of office on that passage of Holy Writ wherein it is asked: "What doth the Lord require of thee but to do justly, and to love mercy, and to walk humbly with thy God?" This I plight to God and country.

Ours has been a favored nation in the bounty which God has bestowed upon it. The great trial of humanity, though indeed we bore our part as well as we were able, left us comparatively little scarred. It is for us to recognize that we have been thus favored, and when we gather at our altars to offer up thanks, we will do well to pledge, in humility and all sincerity, our purpose to prove deserving. We have been raised up and preserved in national power and consequence, as part of a plan whose wisdom we cannot question. Thus believing, we can do no less than hold our nation the willing instrument of the Providence which has so wonderfully favored us. Opportunity for very great service awaits us if we shall prove equal to it. Let our prayers be raised, for direction in the right paths. Under God, our responsibility is great; to our own first, to all men afterward; to all mankind in God's own justice.

—THANKSGIVING PROCLAMATION, OCTOBER 31, 1921

30TH

CALVIN COOLIDGE

1923–1929

We should humbly pray that we may be worthy of a continuation of Divine favor.

Taking over for the suddenly-deceased President Harding, the Vermont-born lawyer worked to restore trust to the Oval Office. He spoke little, dealt forthrightly, and created a favorable business climate. By cutting high wartime taxes, streamlining government operations, and reducing the federal budget by 35 percent, he presided over the "Roaring 20s." Coolidge easily won a full term in 1924, beating his two opponents by more votes than theirs combined. He chose not to run in 1928.

In its main features the Declaration of Independence is a great spiritual document. It is a declaration not of material but of spiritual conceptions. Equality, liberty, popular sovereignty, the rights of man these are not elements which we can see and touch. They are ideals. They have their source and their roots in the religious convictions. They belong to the unseen world. Unless the faith of the American people in these religious convictions is to endure, the principles of our Declaration will perish. We cannot continue to enjoy the result if we neglect and abandon the cause.

—The Inspiration of the Declaration of Independence, July 5, 1926

Harris & Ewing photograph of Calvin Coolidge throwing out the first pitch at the 1924 World Series.

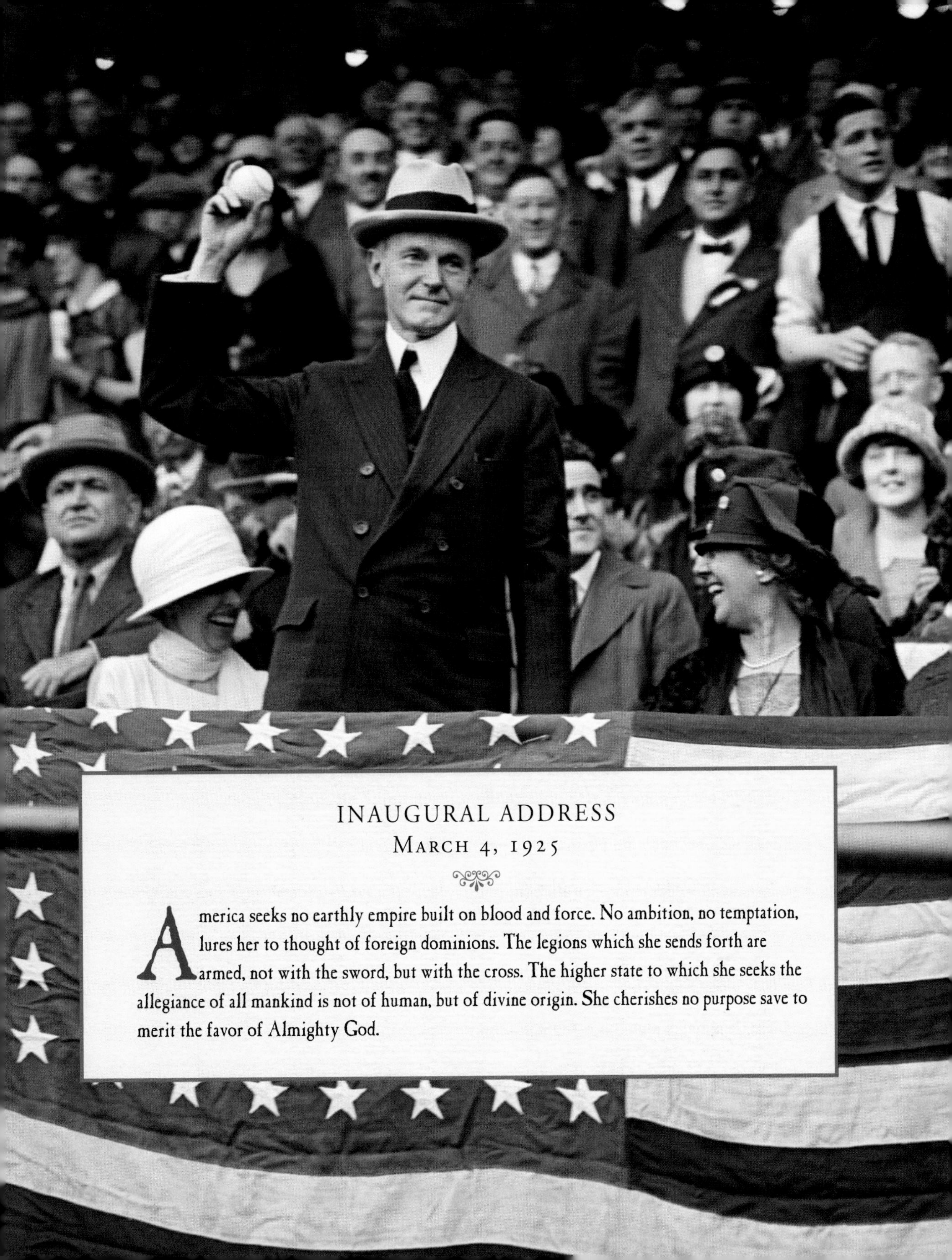

INAUGURAL ADDRESS

MARCH 4, 1925

America seeks no earthly empire built on blood and force. No ambition, no temptation, lures her to thought of foreign dominions. The legions which she sends forth are armed, not with the sword, but with the cross. The higher state to which she seeks the allegiance of all mankind is not of human, but of divine origin. She cherishes no purpose save to merit the favor of Almighty God.

31ST

HERBERT HOOVER

1929–1933

WE HAVE BEEN BLEST WITH DISTINCTIVE EVIDENCE OF DIVINE FAVOR.

After a distinguished career in engineering and overseas humanitarian work, Hoover served as Secretary of Commerce under Presidents Harding and Coolidge. Coming off the successful Republican administration of his predecessor, Hoover swept the electoral college by a margin of 444 to 87. His campaign slogan promised "a chicken for every pot and a car in every garage," but less than eight months later Black Tuesday crashed the stock market and the nation plunged into the Great Depression. His presidency would never recover.

INAUGURAL ADDRESS
MARCH 4, 1929

This occasion is not alone the administration of the most sacred oath which can be assumed by an American citizen. It is a dedication and consecration under God to the highest office in service of our people. I assume this trust in the humility of knowledge that only through the guidance of Almighty Providence can I hope to discharge its ever-increasing burdens. . . .

The problems of the next few years are not only economic. They are also moral and spiritual. The present check to our material success must deeply stir our national conscience upon the purposes of life itself. It must cause us to revalue and reshape our drift from materialism to a higher note of individual and national ideals.

Underlying every purpose is the spiritual application of moral ideals which are the fundamental basis of happiness in a people. This is a land of homes, churches, schoolhouses dedicated to the sober and enduring satisfactions of family life and the rearing of children in an atmosphere of ideals and religious faith. Only with these high standards can we hold society together, and only from them can government survive or business prosper. They are the sole insurance to the safety of our children and the continuity of the nation.

—Presidential Nomination Address, August 11, 1932

The Birthplace of Herbert Hoover, West Branch, Iowa, 1931 *by Grant Wood.*

32ND

FRANKLIN D. ROOSEVELT

1933–1945

RELIGION, BY TEACHING MAN HIS RELATIONSHIP TO GOD, GIVES THE INDIVIDUAL A SENSE OF HIS OWN DIGNITY AND TEACHES HIM TO RESPECT HIMSELF BY RESPECTING HIS NEIGHBORS.

Facing the worst economic crisis in American history, the former New York governor was the only president to be elected four times. Despite his efforts to pull the country out of depression, the malaise dragged on through his first two terms until the nation was thrust into war on December 7, 1941. As Commander-in-Chief, he helped lead the Allies to victory, though he suffered a massive stroke before the war ended, passing away on April 14, 1945.

In this dedication of a Nation we humbly ask the blessing of God. May He protect each and every one of us. May He guide me in the days to come.

—FIRST INAUGURAL ADDRESS, MARCH 4, 1933

Eleanor, Franklin, and son James Roosevelt, with Vice President-elect John Nance Garner on inauguration day,

This nation has placed its destiny in the hands and heads and hearts of its millions of free men and women; and its faith in freedom under the guidance of God.

—Annual Message to Congress on the State of the Union, January 6, 1941

Almighty God: Our sons, pride of our Nation, this day have set upon a mighty endeavor, a struggle to preserve our Republic, our religion, and our civilization, and to set free a suffering humanity. Lead them straight and true; give strength to their arms, stoutness to their hearts, steadfastness in their faith.

They will need Thy blessings. Their road will be long and hard. For the enemy is strong. He may hurl back our forces. Success may not come with rushing speed, but we shall return again and again; and we know that by Thy grace, and by the righteousness of our cause, our sons will triumph.

They will be sore tried, by night and by day, without rest—until the victory is won. The darkness will be rent by noise and flame. Men's souls will be shaken with the violence of war. For these men are lately drawn from the ways of peace. They fight not for the lust of conquest. They fight to end conquest. They fight to liberate. They fight to let justice arise, and tolerance and good will among all Thy people. They yearn but for the end of battle, for their return to the haven of home.

Some will never return. Embrace these, Father, and receive them, Thy heroic servants, into Thy kingdom.

And for us at home—fathers, mothers, children, wives, sisters, and brothers of brave men overseas—whose thoughts and prayers are ever with them—help us, Almighty God, to rededicate ourselves in renewed faith in Thee in this hour of great sacrifice.

Above: American troops head for Omaha Beach June 6, 1944.
Following pages: Self Portrait Among Church Goers *by Ben Shahn, 1939.*

Many people have urged that I call the Nation into a single day of special prayer. But because the road is long and the desire is great, I ask that our people devote themselves in a continuance of prayer. As we rise to each new day, and again when each day is spent, let words of prayer be on our lips, invoking Thy help to our efforts.

Give us strength, too – strength in our daily tasks, to redouble the contributions we make in the physical and the material support of our armed forces. And let our hearts be stout, to wait out the long travail, to bear sorrows that may come, to impart our courage unto our sons wheresoever they may be.

And, O Lord, give us Faith. Give us Faith in Thee; Faith in our sons; Faith in each other; Faith in our united crusade. Let not the keenness of our spirit ever be dulled. Let not the impacts of temporary events, of temporal matters of but fleeting moment let not these deter us in our unconquerable purpose.

With Thy blessing, we shall prevail over the unholy forces of our enemy. Help us to conquer the apostles of greed and racial arrogancies. Lead us to the saving of our country, and with our sister Nations into a world unity that will spell a sure peace a peace invulnerable to the schemings of unworthy men. And a peace that will let all of men live in freedom, reaping the just rewards of their honest toil.

Thy will be done, Almighty God. Amen.

—D-Day Prayer, June 6, 1944

FOURTH INAUGURAL ADDRESS
January 20, 1945

The Almighty God has blessed our land in many ways. He has given our people stout hearts and strong arms with which to strike mighty blows for freedom and truth. He has given to our country a faith which has become the hope of all peoples in an anguished world.

So we pray to Him now for the vision to see our way clearly—to see the way that leads to a better life for ourselves and for all our fellow men—to the achievement of His will to peace on earth.

Church of
IS THE
GOVERNMENT
FOSTERING
IRRELIGION
IN ART
??????

33RD

HARRY S. TRUMAN

1945 - 1953

THIS IS THE HOUR TO REDEDICATE OURSELVES TO THE FAITH IN GOD THAT GIVES US CONFIDENCE AS WE FACE THE CHALLENGE OF THE YEARS AHEAD.

After President Roosevelt's unexpected death only eighty-two days into his fourth term, Vice-President Truman was sworn in as the nations' thirty-third president. His immediate concern was ensuring the surrender of Germany and gaining victory over Japan. After making the monumental decision to drop atomic bombs on Hiroshima and Nagasaki, the Japanese surrendered and reconstruction began. However, his troubles continued as the Soviet Union meddled in Europe and Asia. In his second term, Truman ordered military action in Korea. He chose not to run for another term before the "limited conflict" came to an end.

At this moment, I have in my heart a prayer. As I have assumed my heavy duties, I humbly pray Almighty God, in the words of King Solomon:

"Give therefore thy servant an understanding heart to judge thy people, that I may discern between good and bad; for who is able to judge this thy so great a people?"

I ask only to be a good and faithful servant of my Lord and my people.

—JOINT SESSION OF THE CONGRESS, APRIL 16, 1945

INAUGURAL ADDRESS
January 20, 1949

The American people stand firm in the faith which has inspired this Nation from the beginning. We believe that all men have a right to equal justice under law and equal opportunity to share in the common good. We believe that all men have the right to freedom of thought and expression. We believe that all men are created equal because they are created in the image of God. From this faith we will not be moved....

Steadfast in our faith in the Almighty, we will advance toward a world where man's freedom is secure. To that end we will devote our strength, our resources, and our firmness of resolve. With God's help, the future of mankind will be assured in a world of justice, harmony, and peace.

Whereas from the earliest days of our history our people have been accustomed to turn to Almighty God for help and guidance; and

Whereas in times of national crisis when we are striving to strengthen the foundations of peace and security we stand in special need of divine support; and . . .

Whereas I deem it fitting that this Day of Prayer coincide with the anniversary of the adoption of the Declaration of Independence, which published to the world this Nation's "firm reliance on the protection of Divine Providence":

Now, Therefore, I, Harry S. Truman, President of the United States of America, do hereby proclaim Friday, July 4, 1952, as a National Day of Prayer, on which all of us, in our churches, in our homes, and in our hearts, may beseech God to grant us wisdom to know the course which we should follow, and strength and patience to pursue that course steadfastly. May we also give thanks to Him for His constant watchfulness over us in every hour of national prosperity and national peril.

—National Day of Prayer Proclamation, June 17, 1952

My faith has never been easy for me and never without its obstacles. They say the Hippocratic Oath is about privacy but it's also about the burden of seeing things ordinary people wouldn't like to see. As a medical student and then as a physician, I have struggled and continue to struggle with understanding God's role in inexplicable diseases like terminal tumors in children.

As I wrote in *Taking a Stand: Moving Beyond Partisan Politics To Unite America*, my first patient as a medical student on the surgical service was a beautiful young woman about my age with metastatic melanoma to her ovaries. Though I still had much to learn then about medicine, I knew enough to know her time left on Earth was very short. How could a tragedy like this occur in a world that was supposed to have purpose and design? Where is God's hand when bad things happen to innocent people?

I was very close to my maternal grandmother, Carol Creed Wells. We spent hours in each other's company looking at mint marks on the coins we collected together. But as the years went by, I watched as Gram's sight dimmed until she was diagnosed with macular degeneration. Why does God place such a burden on the elderly? Why are those who lived hard-working, God-fearing lives subjected to the worst pain and torment at the end of them? Tell me the sense in Alzheimer's disease? Tell me God's purpose in taking the only thing that makes life worthwhile from those who have so little left? Why would a loving God take Gram's sight? I wondered.

As many of you know, I became an ophthalmologist partly because of my grandmother's condition. And, although I might not have fully realized it then, God had already begun to answer some of my questions. It's only in looking back that my career as a physician is filled with His light.

Many years ago Kelley gave me a very special gift. She calligraphed some of my favorite Helen Keller quotes along with photos of her and had them framed. For years, they hung in my ophthalmology office. Helen Keller is one of my personal heroes. I've always admired her strength, faith, and refusal to let her spirit, dreams and goals be confined by her physical limitations. The quotes not only inspired me but my patients. Today they hang in my senate office. Here's one:

"I can see, and that is why I can be happy, in what you call the dark, but which to me is golden. . . . I can see a God made world, not a man-made world."

As a physician, I was taught first to do no harm. To think before you act. To analyze the unintended consequences of your actions. I'm still bound to the man-made world in many ways.

But there are times when it's impossible not to believe that there exists something greater even than medicine.

In medical school and later in practice, I've been called on often to examine the eyes of premature babies in neonatal care. I've held a one-pound infant in my hand. I will tell you this with every ounce of my conviction: It is impossible to do so and not believe in the sanctity of life. I've looked into a tiny infant's eyes and have seen God's light.

Leaders of the Big Three at the Potsdam Conference, August 1, 1945. Front row, left to right: Prime Minister Clement Attlee, President Harry S. Truman, General Joseph Stalin. Back row, left to right: Admiral William Leahy, Ernest Bevin, James F. Byrnes, and Vyacheslav Molotov.

34TH

DWIGHT D. EISENHOWER

1953 ~ 1961

UNDER GOD, WE ESPOUSE THE CAUSE OF FREEDOM AND JUSTICE AND PEACE FOR ALL PEOPLES.

Entering office during war time, the popular World War II general secured an armistice seven months into his first term. Domestically, President Eisenhower continued much of the New Deal and Fair Deal of Roosevelt and Truman. He also oversaw the desegregation of the military and sent troops to forcibly desegregate schools in Arkansas. As the cold war frosted over, Eisenhower pursued a policy of peace through strength to maintain world peace. He retired after his second term.

I can't think of Eisenhower without recalling his warnings about the military industrial state. The warnings held so much power then and even today because of Eisenhower's stature as a General and President who knew first hand of the potential for waste in the Pentagon.

> *"In the councils of government, we must guard against the acquisition of unwarranted influence, whether sought or unsought, by the military industrial complex. The potential for the disastrous rise of misplaced power exists and will persist. . . . We must never let the weight of this combination endanger our liberties or democratic processes. We should take nothing for granted. Only an alert and knowledgeable citizenry can compel the proper meshing of the huge industrial and military machinery of defense with our peaceful methods and goals, so that security and liberty may prosper together."*
>
> — FAREWELL ADDRESS TO THE NATION JANUARY 17, 1961

At the end of his military career, Eisenhower said, "I am the most intensely religious man I know. Nobody goes through six years of war without faith." His faith and his views were greatly influenced by Billy Graham, with whom he shared a close relationship.

I don't know if Billy Graham was thinking of Eisenhower when he wrote of courage but I love his description: "Courage is contagious. When a brave man takes a stand, the spine of others are often stiffened."

Eisenhower sought out and listened to Billy Graham. When he was faced with the ominous decision of sending federal troops to enforce desegregation in Arkansas, Eisenhower looked to Graham for advice.

Graham met with every American President since World War II. Graham prayed for and gave advice to more Presidents than any other Pastor in America. According to Graham, "Eisenhower was the first President that really asked my counsel in depth when he was sending troops into Little Rock."

Graham led the fight for integration by example, inviting people of all races to his revivals and crusades starting in 1953. He preached with Martin Luther King, Jr. at a revival in New York City in 1957. Indeed, Graham was instrumental in bailing King out of jail when he was arrested for holding civil rights demonstrations.

When I think of Eisenhower, I also picture Graham preaching. Before I was born, in 1957, Graham's crusade in Madison Square Garden lasted 16 weeks. I remember as a ten-year-old being fascinated by the pictures of Billy Graham preaching to over a million people in South Korea. Two of my favorite Graham quotes are:

> *"The framers of our Constitution meant we were to have freedom of religion, not freedom from religion."*
>
> *"Being a Christian is more than just an instantaneous conversion—it is a daily process whereby you grow to be more and more like Christ."*

I've always been one who objects to easy solutions to complex problems. Like Billy

Reverend Billy Graham with Dwight Eisenhower.

U.S.
U.S.

Graham's quote above I see salvation as an ongoing process. In my life it hasn't always been an easy course without obstacles.

In Walker Percy's novels, he often describes individuals not wholly saved nor wholly lost. In *The Second Coming*, the protagonist Will Barrett describes how lost he is:

> *"Not once in his entire life had he allowed himself to come to rest in the quiet center of himself but had forever cast himself forward from some dark past he could not remember to a future which did not exist. Not once had he been present for his life. So life had passed him like a dream." (p.122)*

Barrett asks, "Is it possible for people to miss their lives in the same way one misses a plane?" I like the way Percy phrases it. Is it possible for something so profoundly wrong to happen—missing one's life—just as if one had overslept and missed a plane? Could something so momentous be wrong, yet still occur amidst the banal and mundaneness of ordinary life?

Will Barrett is lost as so many of our time are lost. His life is in such perpetual motion that it passed him by. Barrett is not a simple character either wholly lost or wholly saved. To the end he still seeks redemption though he remains a little fuzzy if not confused about where to find salvation.

Barrett struggles between polar extremes of the path his dad chose—suicide or the path of religious salvation. He wonders "Is there another way? People either believe everything or they believe nothing." (p.132) He laments as he does in *The Moviegoer* that there doesn't seem to be a place for the seeker. Someone who has not yet found salvation but is still looking.

In my youthful insolence and arrogance, I sometimes chose to dwell and even wallow in the sad and unfortunate circumstances of life, the two-year-old dying from brain cancer or the twenty-two-year-old dying from metastatic melanoma. Over time, I've come to push the pain of death and dying into a corner, neatly and sanitarily secluded from general perusal. Marriage and the miracle of life have allowed me to see Michelangelo's "angel in the stone" not the demon sometimes visible in our daily existence.

Major General Dwight Eisenhower at his desk in 1942.

FIRST INAUGURAL ADDRESS
JANUARY 20, 1953

My friends, before I begin the expression of those thoughts that I deem appropriate to this moment, would you permit me the privilege of uttering a little private prayer of my own. And I ask that you bow your heads:

Almighty God, as we stand here at this moment my future associates in the executive branch of government join me in beseeching that Thou will make full and complete our dedication to the service of the people in this throng, and their fellow citizens everywhere.

Give us, we pray, the power to discern clearly right from wrong, and allow all our words and actions to be governed thereby, and by the laws of this land. Especially we pray that our concern shall be for all the people regardless of station, race, or calling.

May cooperation be permitted and be the mutual aim of those who, under the concepts of our Constitution, hold to differing political faiths; so that all may work for the good of our beloved country and Thy glory. Amen.

In common with religious people everywhere, we in America know that the true cure for the tensions that threaten and too often produce war lies not in guns and bombs but in the spirits and minds of men. We are firm in the belief that faith is the mightiest force that man has at his command. On September twenty-second, we are therefore observing, with an act of faith, a national day of prayer. Throughout the United States of America, whatever our ancestry, whatever our religious affiliation, we shall offer simultaneously to the Almighty our personal prayers for the devotion, wisdom and stamina to work unceasingly for a just and lasting peace for all mankind.

I most earnestly hope that men and women, boys and girls over all the world will join us on that day in that act of faith. May the many millions of people shut away from contact and communion with peoples of the free world join their prayers with ours. May the world be ringed with an act of faith so strong as to annihilate the cruel, artificial barriers erected by little men between the peoples who seek peace on earth through the Divine Spirit.

—STATEMENT BY THE PRESIDENT, SEPTEMBER 21, 1954

35TH

JOHN F. KENNEDY

1961 - 1963

LET US THEREFORE PROCLAIM OUR GRATITUDE TO PROVIDENCE FOR MANIFOLD BLESSINGS.

As the nation entered a new decade, the eloquent and dynamic Congressman from Massachusetts won the Democratic nomination and narrowly defeated Eisenhower's vice president, Richard Nixon. He was both the youngest man elected president and the first Roman Catholic in the Oval Office. His aggressive promotion of civil rights won him both friends and enemies. His handling of the Cuban missile crisis and the failed Bay of Pigs invasion marked a new era in the Cold War as the world dealt with an ever-increasing Soviet menace. His term was cut short on November 22, 1963, when he was assassinated while riding in a motorcade in Dallas, Texas.

I was born in January of 1963. The civil rights movement was in full bloom. All I know of the strife is second-hand. In fact, as I grew up I encountered virtually no evidence of the great struggle for equality. Nevertheless, I am drawn to understand what happened just as I was getting started in life.

A few months after I was born, Clyde Kennard was released from prison. Clyde Kennard is not the most well-known of the civil rights heroes but his story bears retelling. All Clyde wanted was an education, but being black in Mississippi in the 1950s nothing came easy. Instead of getting into college, Clyde got into trouble. He was imprisoned for the crime of wanting an education.

The first time he tried to enroll at Mississippi Southern, the police planted liquor on him, jailed and fined him $600.

After his second attempt to enroll at Mississippi Southern he was arrested on trumped up charges of stealing $25 of chicken feed from his repossessed farm.

He was sentenced to seven years in prison. Seven years! For a crime that he didn't commit.

A man of lesser courage or character would have been bitter. Kennard responded from a higher plane. He wrote: "[W]e have no desire for revenge in our hearts. What we want is to be respected as men and women, given an opportunity to compete with you in the great and interesting race of life."

Clyde Kennard did not live to see the triumphs of the civil rights era. He died from cancer just months after he was released from prison. He left this world just days after his friend, Medgar Evans, was murdered.

We've come a long way since then. But when I think of Clyde Kennard, I am reminded of the challenges we still have with criminal injustices in America and I am encouraged to keep talking and working toward solutions.

In Kennedy's time, the strife was about eliminating discrimination from the law. Today, problems remain but in a different form. Ostensibly, the law treats everyone the same regardless of the color of your skin. And yet, there remains a racial disparity in our criminal justice system.

Three out of four people in prison for non-violent crimes are black or brown. Our prisons are bursting with young men and women of color and our communities full of broken families. Yet, studies show that whites use illegal drugs at least as much as African-Americans and Hispanics.

Why are so many young men of color incarcerated?

Because frankly it is easier to arrest and convict poor kids in urban environments. The problem is compounded when federal grants are issued based on conviction rates.

A new study shows that from 1980 to 2000, the number of children with fathers in prison rose from 350,000 to 2.1 million.

There is a cycle of poverty that often leads to drugs, to debt and to prison. In prison, child support can accumulate into the thousands of dollars. Release from prison finds that employers don't want to hire a convicted felon. With few options of real work, the cycle begins again. Some parolees can't keep up with child support payments and are sent back to a form of debtor's prison. Some can't find work and fall back into the bad habits of the drug trade.

This cycle of poverty, drugs and prison destroys communities.

Enough is enough. We should not sit idly by and watch our criminal justice system continue to consume, confine and define our young men.

As a Christian, I believe in redemption and I believe in second chances. Second chances and criminal justice reform will only happen with bi-partisan support.

We've come a long way since 1964 but despite our progress, there are Clyde Kennards today who cannot fully access the franchise because they are handicapped by our educational and judicial systems.

Those who have known injustice should be at the vanguard of the fight to protect our civil liberties. Make no mistake, everyone should defend our civil liberties, but if you are a member of a group that has ever felt the sting of injustice, your voice should be loud and clear.

If you are Jewish or Japanese, or if the color of your skin ever brought injustice to your doorstep, stand tall and defend the Bill of Rights, defend the right to trial by jury.

No one is immune from the misfortune that comes with bias. Minorities are diverse people representing different colors, ideologies and values. A person with African ancestry is called a minority but so is a person who homeschools their children.

Kennedy, our first Catholic President, presided over a necessary but tumultuous time. He is remembered for his leadership in the fight for justice. His words remind us that he relied on his faith in finding direction.

FIRST INAUGURAL ADDRESS
JANUARY 20, 1961

The world is very different now. For man holds in his mortal hands the power to abolish all forms of human poverty and all forms of human life. And yet the same revolutionary beliefs for which our forebears fought are still at issue around the globe—the belief that the rights of man come not from the generosity of the state, but from the hand of God....

And so, my fellow Americans: ask not what your country can do for you—ask what you can do for your country. My fellow citizens of the world: ask not what America will do for you, but what together we can do for the freedom of man.

Finally, whether you are citizens of America or citizens of the world, ask of us the same high standards of strength and sacrifice which we ask of you. With a good conscience our only sure reward, with history the final judge of our deeds, let us go forth to lead the land we love, asking His blessing and His help, but knowing that here on earth God's work must truly be our own.

"It is a good thing to give thanks unto the Lord."

More than three centuries ago, the Pilgrims, after a year of hardship and peril, humbly and reverently set aside a special day upon which to give thanks to God for their preservation and for the good harvest from the virgin soil upon which they had labored. Grave and unknown dangers remained. Yet by their faith and by their toil they had survived the rigors of the harsh New England winter. Hence they paused in their labors to give thanks for the blessings that had been bestowed upon them by Divine Providence.

This year, as the harvest draws near its close and the year approaches its end, awesome perils again remain to be faced. Yet we have, as in the past, ample reason to be thankful for the abundance of our blessings. We are grateful for the blessings of faith and health and strength and for the imperishable spiritual gifts of love and hope. We give thanks, too, for our freedom as a nation; for the strength of our arms and the faith of our friends; for the beliefs and confidence we share; for our determi-

John Jr., Jacqueline, Caroline, and John F. Kennedy in Hyannis Port, August, 1962.

nation to stand firmly for what we believe to be right and to resist mightily what we believe to be base; and for the heritage of liberty bequeathed by our ancestors which we are privileged to preserve for our children and our children's children.

—THANKSGIVING PROCLAMATION, OCTOBER 27, 1961

You and I are charged with obligations to serve the Great Republic in years of great crisis. The problems we face are complex; the pressures are immense, and both the perils and the opportunities are greater than any nation ever faced. In such a time, the limits of mere human endeavor become more apparent than ever. We cannot depend solely on our material wealth, on our military might, or on our intellectual skill or physical courage to see us safely through the seas that we must sail in the months and years to come.

Along with all of these we need faith. We need the faith with which our first settlers crossed the sea to carve out a state in the wilderness, a mission they said in the Pilgrims' Compact, the Mayflower Compact, undertaken for the glory of God. We need the faith with which our Founding Fathers proudly proclaimed the independence of this country to what seemed at that time an almost hopeless struggle, pledging their lives, their fortunes, and their sacred honor with a firm reliance on the protection of divine providence. We need the faith which has sustained and guided this Nation for 175 long and short years. We are all builders of the future, and whether we build as public servants or private citizens, whether we build at the national or the local level, whether we build in foreign or domestic affairs, we know the truth of the ancient Psalm, "Except the Lord build the house, they labour in vain that build it."

This morning we pray together; this evening apart. But each morning and each evening, let us remember the advice of my fellow Bostonian, the Reverend Phillips Brooks: "Do not pray for easy lives. Pray to be stronger men! Do not pray for tasks equal to your powers. Pray for powers equal to your tasks."

—PRESIDENTIAL PRAYER BREAKFAST, FEBRUARY 7, 1963

An entire generation of people still remember where they were when they heard that Kennedy died. One day, nearly forty years after the assassination, I found myself having lunch with my mom and dad and a potential supporter in Nashville. The man was about my dad's age and the conversation began as so many do among those who've served in the military. The man said to my father: "I served in the Air Force." My father responded that he had served as an Air Force flight surgeon. "Where?" My father explained that he had been stationed at Kelly Air Force Base in San Antonio. A lightbulb seemed to come to the man's face. "What years?" My dad replied "1963–1966." The man's face lit up. "Where were you when you heard that Kennedy had been shot?" My dad remembered the day with detail. He had ridden his bike to work that morning, and as he walked into the clinic a nurse told him through tears that the President had been shot. They had no radio or television so my dad explained, "I went back out into the parking lot to see if I could listen to the news on someone's car radio. There was a guy in the parking lot listening to the radio and I got in his car and we listened together for a good while."

The man looked across the table from us and blurted out, "That was me! I was the guy with the car idling listening to the radio." They were both astonished at the chance meeting that reunited them more than forty years after that mournful day, when they sat in a car together in stunned silence, hearing the tragic news of Kennedy's assassination.

In the aftermath of Kennedy's assassination, the nation grieved. But as my father's story illustrates, Americans came together in their shared pain. We comforted each other and lifted one another up, and the memory of suffering and overcoming are indelibly printed on every person old enough to remember that terrible day, just as are our memories of September 11. When I think of how our country became one united spirit following that tragedy, of our collective gratitude for our courageous police, firefighters, medical and other first responders, I am reminded of this verse from Thessalonians, chapter 5:11, "So encourage each other and give each other strength, just as you are doing now."

36TH

LYNDON B. JOHNSON

1963–1969

LET US GIVE THANKS TO THE ONE WHO GOVERNS US ALL.

Despite being the most formidable enemy of Kennedy in the Democrat primaries, the Texas senator was selected to balance the ticket in 1962. With Kennedy's assassination, Johnson became the thirty-sixth president. His Great Society program birthed numerous government initiatives and bureaucracies to address poverty, health care, crime, education, civil rights, space exploration, and other domestic issues. At the same time, he battled the ongoing Soviet expansion as Americans fought the Communists in Vietnam.

LBJ was a legislator extraordinaire, considered a bigot by some biographers but a man capable of putting together the coalition that finally allowed the Civil Rights Act.

He was also a man driven from office by his complete lack of regard for the tragedy of war and by his inept bungling expansion of the war.

There is a Nepalese proverb: When facing two paths, if you are strong enough, always choose the hardest one. I don't think LBJ sufficiently appreciated how hard the path is that war forces upon our heroes.

Sgt. JD Williams faced two paths and he chose the hardest one.

In a feat of heroism few will ever contemplate, JD, who lives not far from me in Bowling Green, absorbed the blast of an IED that left him a triple amputee.

Afterwards, he said simply, "I'm glad it was me. I was strong enough to withstand

Above: President Johnson meets with Martin Luther King and other civil rights leaders, January 1965.
Below: Johnson shakes hands with Martin Luther King at the signing of the Voting Rights Act, August 1965.

the blast." Amazing words from a hero who lost three limbs and whose heart stopped twice in the field.

In all likelihood he was right, his densely muscled body withstood a blast that would have killed most other men. JD Williams is a hero and an amazingly resilient person.

When I talk with him, he is hopeful. He is a father and a husband and a proud American.

The discussion over war should require men who understand JD's sacrifice for his country and make sure war is not entered into without due consideration for JD and his fellow soldiers.

My wife Kelley, through her work with an organization called Helping a Hero and some true patriots in Bowling Green, helped build a home for JD and his family that would allow him complete mobility and independence from the kitchen design and layout to the bathrooms.

The builder, Bennie Jones, is an incredibly generous Christian man who donated his services as a general contractor. Together with Larkin Ritter, businessman Fred Higgins, and hundreds of people in Bowling Green, they worked to build a home that would meet Sgt. Williams' needs.

One day when Kelley was out at the house with Bennie, when it was nearly complete, he told her that many of the contract laborers, the guys who worked in the hot sun putting the roof tiles on, the bricklayers, painters, and tile setters, refused payment for their work even though the organization had raised plenty of money to pay them. Bennie said they would say, "No, please just tell Sgt. Williams I'm praying for him and his family. Use the money for the next soldier that needs it." Bennie told her, "Kelley, I feel like God's hands are all over this house." And standing there, she felt it, too. It was the work of God through the hands of people from all walks of life who wanted to show their love and appreciation for a 25-year-old soldier and his young wife and daughter. The singer Lee Greenwood was there when we celebrated giving the keys to the house to Sgt. Williams. He sang his hit "God Bless the USA" and tears filled all of our eyes.

LBJ sought God's guidance as he made the fateful decision to expand the war in Vietnam. In his 1963 Thanksgiving address he acknowledged man's weakness. Five years later as the Vietnam War raged and American soldiers died he asked God's help for all men to live in peace but he failed to take any action that might have helped bring about that peace.

Tonight, on this Thanksgiving, I come before you to ask your help, to ask your strength, to ask your prayers that God may guard this Republic and guide my every labor. . . .

Let us today renew our dedication to the ideals that are American. Let us pray for His divine wisdom in banishing from our land any injustice or intolerance or oppression to any of our fellow Americans whatever their opinion, whatever the color of their skins—for God made all of us, not some of us, in His image. All of us, not just some of us, are His children.

—Thanksgiving Address November 28, 1963

Above the pyramid on the Great Seal of the United States it says in Latin, "God has favored our undertaking." God will not favor everything that we do. It is rather our duty to divine His will.

—Civil Rights Speech, March 15, 1965

Ever since I visited Ferguson, Baltimore, Philadelphia, and the Southside of Chicago I have been saying there is an undercurrent of unease in our country. There is a tension that has become visible in the protests in every major American city.

The turmoil that erupted in LBJ's time has abated but there continues to be a discontent that seems to be just one incident away from erupting again.

Following pages: Amen, *2010 by Laura James.*

Scarred by the weaknesses of man, with whatever guidance God may offer us, we must nevertheless and alone with our mortality, strive to ennoble the life of man on earth.

— Lyndon B. Johnson, State of the Union address, January 12, 1966

37TH

RICHARD M. NIXON

1969 - 1974

MAY GOD GIVE US THE WISDOM, THE STRENGTH AND, ABOVE ALL, THE IDEALISM . . .

Despite previous political losses, the former Navy lieutenant, U.S. Senator, and Vice President captured the Republican nomination again in 1968. In a three-way race, he defeated Democrat Hubert Humphrey and Democrat-turned-Independent George Wallace. His adroitness in foreign affairs helped end hostilities in Vietnam and improve relations with the Soviet Union and China. At home, he ended the draft, reduced crime, and passed sweeping environmental reform. He was easily re-elected in 1972, crushing his opponent in the electoral college 520 to 17. However, a re-election scandal at the now-notorious Watergate Hotel consumed his administration and on August 8, 1974, President Nixon became the first American president to resign the office.

Nixon was in office when the Supreme Court handed down *Roe v. Wade* the fateful decision that legalized abortion in the United States.

That decision still haunts many of us who believe in the sanctity of life. I like the way Senator John East described that specialness as "the majesty and mystery of creation."

When I arrived in Washington, I was asked to speak at the March for Life where tens of thousands of pro-life supporters gather on the Capitol mall to remember the anniversary of *Roe v. Wade.*

As a physician, I take seriously my oath to First, do no harm. I have treated one and two-pound babies in the neonatal intensive care unit for retinopathy prematurity, always aware that the tiny human in my care was a precious life, fighting for its chance, an individual with abilities and potential that I could only wonder about.

I never lost my sense of awe for the new individual in my care, my sense of responsibility for its future. Would this tiny one hold the key to discoveries in science, medicine, exploration? Would this fragile human being shine in the world of the arts, bringing beauty and inspiration?

Virtually every family in America is touched by children born with disabilities and special needs. It is hard for me to fathom that some people argue that the least among us somehow deserve less rights than others.

I believe that all human life is special and deserves protection.

I cannot help but see "the majesty and mystery of creation."

I don't think that a civilization can long endure that does not have respect for life, born and not yet born. I believe that rhetoric and platitudes have so dumbed down the debate that the thorny issue of "When does life begin?" has been lost in the shuffle. When both sides decide to honestly examine and really ponder the significance of that question, maybe a more thoughtful debate will ensue.

In Nixon's first inaugural address, nearly a half century ago, he began the debate: "I am here in the cold with you today. And I say we should keep on marching until the time comes that our great nation chooses again to respect, revere, and defend all human life."

When Nixon accepted the nomination in the summer of 1968, he acknowledged the challenge of "restoring peace."

Richard Nixon at Robbins AFB, November 1973.

One hundred and eight years ago, the newly elected President of the United States, Abraham Lincoln, left Springfield, Illinois, never to return again. He spoke to his friends gathered at the railroad station. Listen to his words:

"Today I leave you. I go to assume a greater task than devolved on General Washington. The great God which helped him must help me. Without that great assistance, I will surely fail. With it, I cannot fail."

Abraham Lincoln lost his life but he did not fail.

The next President of the United States will face challenges which in some ways will be greater than those of Washington or Lincoln. Because for the first time in our nation's history, an American President will face not only the problem of restoring peace abroad but of restoring peace at home.

Without God's help and your help, we will surely fail; but with God's help and your help, we shall surely succeed.

My fellow Americans, the long dark night for America is about to end.

The time has come for us to leave the valley of despair and climb the mountain so that we may see the glory of the dawn—a new day for America, and a new dawn for peace and freedom in the world.

—Presidential Nomination Acceptance Speech, August 8, 1968

FIRST INAUGURAL ADDRESS
January 20, 1969

We are caught in war, wanting peace. We are torn by division, wanting unity. We see around us empty lives, wanting fulfillment. We see tasks that need doing, waiting for hands to do them. To a crisis of the spirit, we need an answer of the spirit. . . .

Our destiny offers, not the cup of despair, but the chalice of opportunity. So let us seize it, not in fear, but in gladness—and, "riders on the earth together," let us go forward, firm in our faith, steadfast in our purpose, cautious of the dangers; but sustained by our confidence in the will of God and the promise of man.

38TH

GERALD R. FORD

1974 ~ 1977

MY RELIGIOUS FEELING IS A DEEP PERSONAL FAITH I RELY ON FOR GUIDANCE FROM MY GOD.

When Vice President Spiro Agnew resigned in 1973 after facing charges of tax evasion, President Nixon tapped the House Minority Leader to replace him. A year later, the president himself resigned, elevating the former Congressman to leader of the free world. Once in office, President Ford pursued a moderate domestic agenda, conservative fiscal policies, and peace internationally. He lost his only presidential election to the Governor of Georgia, but when Jimmy Carter took office, he began his inaugural speech by declaring, "I want to thank my predecessor for all he has done to heal our land."

I now solemnly reaffirm my promise I made to you last December 6: to uphold the Constitution, to do what is right as God gives me to see the right, and to do the very best I can for America. God helping me, I will not let you down.

—REMARKS UPON TAKING THE OATH OF OFFICE AS PRESIDENT, AUGUST 9, 1974

Gerald Ford and Liberty in the Oval Office, November 1974.

I have heard many inspiring Presidential speeches, but the words I remember best were spoken by Dwight D. Eisenhower. "America is not good because it is great," the President said. "America is great because it is good."

President Eisenhower was raised in a poor but religious home in the heart of America. His simple words echoed President Lincoln's eloquent testament that "right makes might." And Lincoln in turn evoked the silent image of George Washington kneeling in prayer at Valley Forge.

So, all these magic memories which link eight generations of Americans are summed up in the inscription just above me. How many times have we seen it? "In God We Trust." Let us engrave it now in each of our hearts as we begin our Bicentennial.

—State of the Union Address, January 19, 1976

We are gathered here this morning to recall and to renew that faith—faith in God and belief in the future of our country. We seek to sustain and to increase our spiritual strength at this time of prayer and recollection.

John Muhlenburg wrote in his diary in 1776, about 200 years ago: "There is a time to pray and a time to fight. This is the time to fight." If he were alive today and writing in 1976, he may have written, "This is the time to pray."

Let men and women of faith remember that this Nation, endowed by God with so many blessings, is also surrounded by incredible needs. At the beginning of this century in American history, let us remember Jesus, who, surrounded by needs still early in the morning, went away to a solitary place to pray.

—National Prayer Breakfast, January 29, 1976

39TH

JAMES CARTER

1977–1981

I RESORT TO PRAYER THAT MY JUDGMENT WILL BE SOUND AND CONDUCIVE TO PEACE AND JUSTICE.

The former Baptist Sunday School teacher and naval officer climbed the political rungs of his home state of Georgia to become governor. After defeating President Ford, he sought to combat rising inflation and unemployment domestically while pursuing peace internationally. The historic Camp David agreement provided peace between Israel and Egypt. The SALT-II agreement attempted to slow the expansion of nuclear arms, but the Soviet's invasion of Afghanistan in 1979 shattered relations. When the U.S. embassy was overrun in Iran and 52 Americans held hostage for over a year, Republicans rallied to defeat the president's bid for a second term.

I'm not much of a fan of President Jimmy Carter but I'm quite fond of the humanitarian Jimmy Carter. His help and sponsorship for Habitat for Humanity helped a great charity to succeed.

I also respect him as a man of faith who publicly questions the use of religion to treat women as inferior.

My own faith journey has not been a straight line. I've had my ups and downs, a few zigs and zags.

Dostoevsky wrote: "I did not arrive at my hosanna through childlike faith but through a fiery furnace of doubt."

In the end, I am faithful to my wife and to my family. I try to be a good Christian, husband and father. I try to adhere to the tenets of the New Testament. I take seriously my oath to defend the Constitution. I fight for truth, as I see it, regardless of the political outcome. I see policy, even our fiscal problems, in terms of morality.

I believe it is immoral to force debt upon future generations. I believe that we have a responsibility to our children and grandchildren to leave them a country at least as good as the country we've enjoyed.

Christianity ultimately is a message of hope. We need leadership that can find hope and optimism amidst the fiscal crisis that we face. We need to find leadership that can transform the coldness of austerity into the warm embrace of prosperity.

I agree with Ralph Reed who often states that the first amendment is to keep government out of religion, not to keep religious people out of government.

We need leadership that will extol the American Dream, that is proud of America, that can convince us to believe in ourselves again. We must first discover who we are before we can lead this country back to greatness.

Political parties are empty vessels unless we imbue them with values. Republicans must first decide who we are—before we lead.

I believe that our nation faces a spiritual crisis that no political leader can or will cure. I believe that a spiritual awakening is necessary in America.

Periodically, throughout history, a need arises for renewal of faith or a spiritual awakening. I believe today's fiscal crisis is somehow related to a moral ambivalence that unchecked threatens our country's future.

Our country faces a dilemma, the fiscal nightmare is evident in the numbers but our dilemma is not just dollars and cents. When you see images of a person beaten to the point of convulsions filmed by workers at a McDonalds who videotaped the cruelty rather than stop the horror, something even more complex than just deficit financing infects our people.

When nine people are murdered in their church in Charleston, South Carolina, something more significant than just our debt and fiscal irresponsibility ails us.

Barton Warren Stone gathered tens of thousands of Christians at Cane Ridge, Kentucky, in 1801 because there was a gathering storm that necessitated a revival. America stands amidst just such a storm with fiscal disaster whirling about out of control and a moral ambivalence that calls out for spiritual renewal.

My hope is that we will as a people and a nation wake up. We owe it to our children and grandchildren to do everything we can to save this great Republic. In that cause, I will do the best that I can.

Thanksgiving Day was first celebrated in this land not in a moment of unbridled triumph, but in times of great adversity. The colonies of Massachusetts and Virginia had few material possessions to help them face the dangers of the wilderness. They had no certainty that the harvests for which they gave thanks would be sufficient to carry,

Jimmy Carter, leads the congregation of Maranatha Baptist Church in prayer on Sunday, June 15, 2014, in Plains, Georgia.

them through a long winter. Yet they gave thanks to God for what they had and for the hope of this new land.

In the darkest hour of the American Revolution, when the young Republic faced defeat by the strongest military power on Earth, our forefathers also saw fit to give thanks for their blessings. In the midst of a devastating Civil War, President Lincoln proclaimed a day to express gratitude for our "singular deliverances and blessings. . . ."

Like those who came before us, we come to give thanks for our singular deliverances and blessings, in a time of both danger and great promise. May we be thankful in proportion to that which we have received, trusting not in our wealth and comforts, but in the strength of our purpose, that all nations might be similarly blessed with liberty and abundance and live in peace.

—Thanksgiving Proclamation, September 28, 1979

Our Nation requires by law that the church and the state must be separated. The church cannot dominate our government. Our government cannot dominate nor influence religion. But there is no way for a human being to separate in one's own heart and mind those inevitable correlations—responsibilities of a secular life, even in government, on the one hand, responsibilities to God on the other. They combine to form what a person is, what a person thinks, what a person hopes to be.

—National Prayer Breakfast, January 18, 1979

We are a community, a beloved community, all of us. Our individual fates are linked, our futures intertwined. And if we act in that knowledge and in that spirit, together, as the Bible says, we can move mountains.

—State of the Union address, January 19, 1978

I call upon all the people of our Nation to give thanks on that day for the blessings Almighty God has bestowed upon us, and to join the fervent prayer of George Washington who as President asked God to ". . . impart all the blessings we possess, or ask for ourselves to the whole family of mankind."

—Thanksgiving Proclamation, November 13, 1980

When Jimmy Carter was elected I was thirteen. My family didn't get too excited one way or the other about the Presidential election as my dad thought Ford only marginally better than Carter. My dad had won a special election to Congress in April of 1976 and I made my first trip to Washington. We didn't move to Washington and my dad was defeated in November of 1976 and not reelected until 1978. But for most of the 1970s my life was more about the small town of Lake Jackson, Texas, than about politics.

In moments of doubt I think of Philippians 4:7: "And the peace of God, which passeth all understanding, shall keep your hearts and minds through Christ Jesus."

The peace that passeth all understanding. I still, in my imperfect way, strive to make sense of man's inhumanity to man, to make sense of the evil around us. The poetry of the language gives permanence to the message and reminds me daily of a goal that exceeds the mundane and surpasses the staid and really can only be described as a "peace that passeth all understanding."

I also always enjoy the doxology:

Praise God, from Whom all blessings flow;
Praise Him, all creatures here below;
Praise Him above, ye heavenly host;
Praise Father, Son, and Holy Ghost.

The words come from a hymn written by Ken Thomas in 1674. No good deed goes unpunished and Ken was imprisoned in the Tower of London for refusing to sign King James II's "Declaration of Indulgence" that would have restored Catholicism in England.

Whenever my mind obsesses over the daily evils present in our world, I try to remember all the good and "praise God, from whom all blessings flow."

40TH

RONALD REAGAN

1981–1989

GOD SHOULD NEVER HAVE BEEN EXPELLED FROM AMERICA'S CLASSROOMS IN THE FIRST PLACE.

Reagan, the actor-turned-governor from California, swept the 1980 elections on a platform of economic recovery and the release of the Iranian hostages. On the day Reagan was inaugurated, Iran released all of the Americans and the balance of world affairs began to shift. His conservative economic policies lowered tax rates, reduced inflation, stimulated employment, and strengthened the economy. In his bid for a second term, his opponent carried only his home state of Minnesota and the Reagan-Bush ticket carried the most electoral votes in American history. As his second term ended, so did the Cold War as the Soviet Union crumbled and its European satellite states broke free. Upon retirement, Reagan returned to Southern California where, after a decade-long battle with Alzheimer's disease, he died on June 5, 2004.

I first met Ronald Reagan when I was a teenager. I went with my family to the Republican National Convention in Kansas City. My dad was a delegate for Reagan. Reagan didn't win that year but he returned the favor and came to Houston to campaign for my dad in 1978. We have a family photo taken with Reagan from that trip. Unfortunately, I'm wearing a rust-colored three-piece corduroy suit—they say all fashion eventually returns. I'm not holding my breath for the return of the corduroy suit.

Nancy and Ronald Reagan in California, August 1964.

FIRST INAUGURAL ADDRESS
JANUARY 20, 1981

I'm told that tens of thousands of prayer meetings are being held on this day, and for that I'm deeply grateful. We are a nation under God, and I believe God intended for us to be free. It would be fitting and good, I think, if on each Inaugural Day in future years it should be declared a day of prayer.

SECOND INAUGURAL ADDRESS
JANUARY 21, 1985

With heart and hand let us stand as one today—one people under God, determined that our future shall be worthy of our past.... Now we're standing inside this symbol of our democracy, and we see and hear again the echoes of our past: a general falls to his knees in the hard snow of Valley Forge; a lonely President paces the darkened halls and ponders his struggle to preserve the Union; the men of the Alamo call out encouragement to each other; a settler pushes west and sings a song, and the song echoes out forever and fills the unknowing air.

It is the American sound. It is hopeful, big-hearted, idealistic, daring, decent, and fair. That's our heritage, that's our song. We sing it still. For all our problems, our differences, we are together as of old. We raise our voices to the God who is the Author of this most tender music. And may He continue to hold us close as we fill the world with our sound—in unity, affection, and love—one people under God, dedicated to the dream of freedom that He has placed in the human heart, called upon now to pass that dream on to a waiting and hopeful world.

Reagan's fame and success are often attributed to his sense of optimism. Who we are and what traits we express are inescapably part of our past. Reagan was no different.

Author Paul Kengor writes of a young Ronald Reagan. It was "a brisk February evening in Dixon, Illinois in 1922. Returning home from a basketball game at the YMCA, 11-year-old Ronald expected to arrive to an empty house. Instead, he was stunned by the sight of his father sprawled out in the snow on the front porch. "He was drunk," his son later remembered. "Dead to the world . . . crucified." [The father's] hair was soaked with melted snow, matted unevenly against the side of his reddened face. The smell of whiskey emanated from his mouth.

Young Reagan stood over his father for a minute or two. He wanted to simply let himself in the door and pretend his dad wasn't there. Instead, he grabbed a fistful of overcoat and heaved [his father] to the bedroom, away from the weather's harm and neighbors' attention."

This young boy became the man—Ronald Reagan—whose sunny optimism and charisma shined so brightly that it cured the malaise of the late seventies, a confidence that beamed so broadly that it pulled us through a serious recession, and a faith that tugged so happily at all hearts that a generation of Democrats became Republicans.

The American Dream is that any among us could become the next Thomas Edison, the next Henry Ford, the next Ronald Reagan. Reagan spoke to that promise that lives in each soul in his prayers for our country.

> *Since her beginning America has held fast to this hope of divine providence, this vision of "man with God." It is true that world peace is jeopardized by those who view man—not as a noble being—but as an accident of nature, without soul, and important only to the extent he can serve an all-powerful state. But it is our spiritual commitment—more than all the military might in the world—that will win our struggle for peace. It is not "bombs and rockets" but belief and resolve—it is humility before God that is ultimately the source of America's strength as a nation. Our people always have held fast to this belief, this vision, since our first days as a nation. . . .*
>
> *Let us resolve tonight that young Americans will always see those Potomac lights; that they will always find there a city of hope in a country that is free. And let us*

President Reagan being sworn in, January 21, 1985.

resolve they will say of our day and our generation that we did keep faith with our God, that we did act "worthy of ourselves;" that we did protect and pass on lovingly that shining city on a hill.

—ELECTION EVE ADDRESS, NOVEMBER 3, 1980

I tell you there are a great many God-fearing, dedicated, noble men and women in public life, present company included. And, yes, we need your help to keep us ever mindful of the ideas and the principles that brought us into the public arena in the first place. The basis of those ideals and principles is a commitment to freedom and personal liberty that, itself, is grounded in the much deeper realization that freedom prospers only where the blessings of God are avidly sought and humbly accepted.

The American experiment in democracy rests on this insight. Its discovery was the great triumph of our Founding Fathers, voiced by William Penn when he said: "If we will not be governed by God, we must be governed by tyrants." Explaining the inalienable rights of men, Jefferson said, "The God who gave us life, gave us liberty at the same time." And it was George Washington who said that "of all the dispositions and habits which lead to political prosperity, religion and morality are indispensable supports."

And finally, that shrewdest of all observers of American democracy, Alexis de Tocqueville, put it eloquently after he had gone on a search for the secret of America's greatness and genius—and he said: "Not until I went into the churches of America and heard her pulpits aflame with righteousness did I understand the greatness and the genius of America. . . . America is good. And if America ever ceases to be good, America will cease to be great."

Well, I'm pleased to be here today with you who are keeping America great by keeping her good. Only through your work and prayers and those of millions of others can we hope to survive this perilous century and keep alive this experiment in liberty, this last, best hope of man.

. . . Freedom prospers when religion is vibrant and the rule of law under God is acknowledged. When our Founding Fathers passed the first amendment, they sought to protect churches from government interference. They never intended to construct a wall of hostility between government and the concept of religious belief itself.

—"EVIL EMPIRE" SPEECH, MARCH 8, 1983

41ST

GEORGE H. W. BUSH

1989 - 1993

TELL THEM WE ARE ONE NATION UNDER GOD.

Riding waves of success, Vice President Bush was elected in a continuance of the Reagan era. The Massachusetts native had served as a naval pilot in World War II, a Congressman from Texas, Ambassador to the United Nations, and Director of the Central Intelligence Agency. As President, he oversaw the end of the Cold War as the Soviet Union disintegrated and the Berlin Wall fell. As threats in the Middle East grew, President Bush thwarted Saddam Hussein's invasion of Kuwait and fought to preserve peace in neighboring volatile regions. At home, the economy faltered and government spending rose. In a bid for re-election, he lost a three-way race by capturing only 37 percent of the vote to his opponents, Governor Bill Clinton and businessman Ross Perot, who won 43 and 19 percent, respectively.

As we pause to acknowledge the kindnesses God has shown to us—and, indeed, His gift of life itself—we do so in a spirit of humility as well as gratitude. When the United States was still a fledgling democracy, President Washington asked the American people to unite in prayer to the "great Lord and ruler of Nations," in order to: beseech him to pardon our national and other Transgressions; to enable us all, whether in public or private Stations, to perform our several and relative Duties properly and punctually; to render our national Government a blessing to all the People, by constantly being a Government of wise, just and constitutional Laws, discreetly and faithfully

Serve the Lord with gladness: come before His presence with singing.

FIRST INAUGURAL ADDRESS
JANUARY 20, 1989

My first act as President is a prayer. I ask you to bow your heads.

Heavenly Father, we bow our heads and thank You for Your love. Accept our thanks for the peace that yields this day and the shared faith that makes its continuance likely. Make us strong to do Your work, willing to heed and hear Your will, and write on our hearts these words: "Use power to help people."

For we are given power not to advance our own purposes, nor to make a great show in the world, nor a name. There is but one just use of power, and it is to serve people. Help us to remember it, Lord. The Lord our God be with us, as He was with our fathers; may He not leave us or forsake us; so that He may incline our hearts to Him, to walk in all His ways . . . that all peoples of the earth may know that the Lord is God; there is no other. . . .

I do not mistrust the future; I do not fear what is ahead. For our problems are large, but our heart is larger. Our challenges are great, but our will is greater. And if our flaws are endless, God's love is truly boundless.

executed and obeyed; to protect and guide all Sovereigns and Nations . . . and to bless them with good Government, peace and Concord.

Today . . . we continue to offer thanks and praise to our Creator, that "Great Author of every public and private good," for the many blessings He has bestowed upon us. In so doing, we recall the timeless words of the 100th Psalm:

Serve the Lord with gladness: come before His presence with singing.

Know ye that the Lord He is God: it is He that hath made us, and not we ourselves; we are His people, and the sheep of His pasture.

Enter into His gates with thanksgiving, and into His courts with praise: be thankful unto Him, and bless His name. For the Lord is good; His mercy is everlasting; and His truth endureth to all generations.

—THANKSGIVING PROCLAMATION, NOVEMBER 17, 1989

The American Church *by Mark Baring.*

42ND

WILLIAM J. CLINTON

1993–2001

. . . ASKING GOD'S BLESSING ON OUR ENDEAVORS AND ON OUR BELOVED COUNTRY.

Bill Clinton was born in the small, rural town of Hope, Arkansas. He excelled in school, earning a Rhodes Scholarship and obtaining his law degree from Yale University. He immediately entered politics in his home state. Within a few short years, he was elected Attorney General. Two years later, he won the Governorship, the first term of several that would total almost twelve years. As President Bush's popularity faded, the energetic young governor defeated the incumbent in a three-way race.

And I would like to say a special word to our religious leaders. You know, I'm proud of the fact the United States has more houses of worship per capita than any country in the world. These people who lead our houses of worship can ignite their congregations to carry their faith into action, can reach out to all of our children, to all of the people in distress, to those who have been savaged by the breakdown of all we hold dear. Because so much of what must be done must come from the inside out and our religious leaders and their congregations can make all the difference, they have a role in the New Covenant as well.

—STATE OF THE UNION, JANUARY 24, 1995

The children of this country can learn in a profound way that integrity is important and selfishness is wrong, but God can change us and make us strong at the broken places. . . .

I ask you to share my prayer that God will search me and know my heart, try me and know my anxious thoughts, see if there is any hurtfulness in me, and lead me toward the life everlasting. I ask that God give me a clean heart, let me walk by faith and not sight.

I ask once again to be able to love my neighbor—all my neighbors—as myself, to be an instrument of God's peace; to let the words of my mouth and the meditations of my heart and, in the end, the work of my hands, be pleasing.

—White House Prayer Breakfast, September 11, 1998

Americans today still cherish the fresh air of freedom, in which we can raise our families and worship God as we choose without fear of persecution. We still rejoice in this great land and in the civil and religious liberty it offers to all. And we still—and always—raise our voices in prayer to God, thanking Him in humility for the countless blessings He has bestowed on our Nation and our people.

—Thanksgiving Proclamation, November 11, 1996

Bill Clinton at a "Get Out the Vote" rally in Los Angeles, November 2, 2000.

43RD

GEORGE W. BUSH

2001–2009

I PRAY FOR A LOT OF THINGS . . . I PRAY FOR STRENGTH, AND I PRAY FOR COMFORT; I PRAY FOR FRIENDS; I PRAY FOR MY FAMILY'S SAFETY. MY RELATIONSHIP WITH THE ALMIGHTY IS A VERY PERSONAL RELATIONSHIP.

The son of the forty-first president, George W. Bush defeated Vice President Albert Gore, Jr. in his effort to extend the Clinton era. Within his first year in office, the nation faced the worst attack on U.S. soil since Pearl Harbor and America was plunged into open war with radical Muslims. Both terms were challenged by the ensuing wars in Afghanistan and Iraq, as well as attempted plots against domestic targets. At home, he focused on education, tax relief, homeland security, and free trade.

I had coffee with George W. in his Dallas office in early 2014. I asked him if his foreign policy could be seen as an extension of his father's foreign policy albeit with the caveat that the attack of 9/11 had forced him to be more aggressive.

He was adamant that his foreign policy was distinct from his father's, that his foreign policy goal was to ambitiously spread freedom and democracy across the planet.

I thought to myself, though, that the events of 9/11 affected us all and surely we wouldn't have gone to war in Iraq if 9/11 hadn't occurred.

No matter what I think of the decisions Bush made as president, I believe he truly loves his country and sincerely cares for the soldiers who valiantly fought.

When I think of the horror of 9/11, I also remember the outpouring of love and unity our country showed, our resolve and gratitude for our brave first responders, and our sense of volunteerism in the face of danger. I think of Frank Silecchia, an ironworker who volunteered for months in the rescue effort and helped pull 47 bodies from the wreckage of the twin towers. One day, fatigued and shattered, he discovered something that caused him to fall on his knees in tears. There in the wreckage, comprised of a 17-foot-steel column and crossbeam, was a cross. "It was a sign," he would later say. "A sign that God hadn't deserted us."

He approached Reverend Brian Jordan, a Franciscan Priest who was praying with rescue workers each day. "You found it. I'll save it," Reverend Jordan told him. Ten days later, the cross was lifted out by crane to stand on the west side of Ground Zero. As bagpipers played "Amazing Grace," Reverend Jordan held a blessing ceremony, saying, "Behold, the glory of the cross at Ground Zero. This is our symbol of hope. This is our symbol of faith. This is our symbol of healing." In the months that followed, Reverend Jordan held mass at the cross, welcoming people of all faiths, or none at all. The numbers grew from dozens to hundreds.

I'm sure Lucky Penney won't ever forget where she was on 9/11.

Lucky Penney was one of the first female F-16 pilots. She was asked to scramble her fighter jet after the first two planes hit the twin towers.

Her mission? To stop Flight 93, now over Pennsylvania, from reaching the White House. Only problem was, we had no fighter jets available that were armed.

Their only recourse would be to ram the plane to destroy it. In essence, a kamikaze or suicide mission. Lucky Penney accepted her assignment and took to the skies in minutes. No time for the usual methodical pre-flight checklists that pilots typically go through. She taxied for the runway as her crew was still detaching equipment from the jet.

Fortunately, she didn't have to give her life to stop that plane. The passengers heroically stopped the evil the hijackers had in mind.

Four days after 9/11, George W. called the nation together at the national prayer breakfast. "God's signs are not always the ones we look for. We learn in tragedy that his purposes are not always our own." Out of that terrible tragedy he asked for God to grant us "patience and resolve."

I believe in a God who calls us, not to judge our neighbors, but to love them. I believe in grace, because I have seen it; in peace, because I have felt it; in forgiveness, because I have needed it.

—Nomination Acceptance Speech, August 3, 2000

Our purpose as a nation is firm, yet our wounds as a people are recent and unhealed and lead us to pray. In many of our prayers this week, there's a searching and an honesty. At St. Patrick's Cathedral in New York, on Tuesday, a woman said, "I pray to God to give us a sign that he's still here." Others have prayed for the same, searching hospital to hospital, carrying pictures of those still missing.

God's signs are not always the ones we look for. We learn in tragedy that his purposes are not always our own, yet the prayers of private suffering, whether in our homes or in this great cathedral are known and heard and understood.

There are prayers that help us last through the day or endure the night. There are prayers of friends and strangers that give us strength for the journey, and there are prayers that yield our will to a will greater than our own. . . . This world He created is of moral design. Grief and tragedy and hatred are only for a time. Goodness, remembrance and love have no end, and the Lord of life holds all who die and all who mourn. . . .

On this national day of prayer and remembrance, we ask almighty God to watch over our nation and grant us patience and resolve in all that is to come. We pray that He will comfort and console those who now walk in sorrow. We thank Him for each life we now must mourn, and the promise of a life to come.

As we've been assured, neither death nor life nor angels nor principalities, nor powers nor things present nor things to come nor height nor depth can separate us from God's love. May He bless the souls of the departed. May He comfort our own. And may He always guide our country.

—National Prayer Service, September 14, 2001

Tonight I ask for your prayers for all those who grieve, for the children whose worlds have been shattered, for all whose sense of safety and security has been threatened. And

I pray they will be comforted by a power greater than any of us, spoken through the ages in Psalm 23: "Even though I walk through the valley of the shadow of death, I fear no evil, for You are with me."

This is a day when all Americans from every walk of life unite in our resolve for justice and peace. America has stood down enemies before, and we will do so this time. None of us will ever forget this day. Yet, we go forward to defend freedom and all that is good and just in our world.

Thank you. Good night, and God bless America.

—Address to the Nation on the Terrorist Attacks, September 11, 2001

Freedom is not America's gift to the world; it is the Almighty God's gift to every man and woman in this world.

—Nomination Acceptance Speech, September 2, 2004

President George W. Bush was always clear to say that the attacks on 9/11 didn't mean that we were at war with Islam. While that is true, it must be acknowledged that a radical aberration of Islam is the common denominator to the attacks.

Ever since 9/11, commentators have tried to avoid pointing fingers at Islam. Rightly, pointing out that most Muslims are not committed to violence against Christians. But this is not the whole truth. True, only a minority of Muslims condone killing of Christians, but that minority numbers in the tens of millions.

Pew Research did a poll which indicated that 21% of Egyptian, 15% of Jordanian, 13% of Pakistani, 6% of Turkish and 2% of Lebanese Muslims find terrorism acceptable if not laudable. A minority to be sure but if you add up the population you find that the percentages in just five countries come to over 47 million Muslims!

The Syrian civil war shows just how messy this worldwide conflict has become. The vast majority of Syrian Christians are allied with Assad. The U.S. and her allies are arming the Islamic rebels fighting Assad. In fact, the former U.S. ambassador to Syria acknowledges that it is inevitable that our arms will fight alongside Al Queda and Al Nusra (and by extension, ISIS) in this violent civil war.

To witness the disastrous results of this civil war one need only travel to Maalula,

Syria, an ancient Christian city where they still speak Aramaic, the language that Jesus spoke. They have been Christian since the time of Christ. They are a small final outpost of Christians in the Middle East. In the summer of 2013, the town was overrun by the Islamic rebels. Rebels, who at the very least are allies of the rebels we are arming, and at the very worst may be armed by the Obama administration.

As the Islamic jihadists swarmed into town they demanded everyone convert to Islam or die. Sarkis el Zakhm stood up and answered them, "I am a Christian and if you want to kill me because I am a Christian, do it." Those were Sarkis' last words. Sister Carmel of Damascus said of Sarkis: "His death is true martyrdom, a death in odium fidei (the hatred of faith)." I wrote about Sarkis el Zakhm in my book *Taking a Stand*, as well as the tragic story of Asia Bibi.

Asia Bibi, a Pakistani Christian, sits on death row for blasphemy. In her memoir, *Blasphemy*, she says it all began when she drew water from a Muslim well. As she was filling her bowl of water, a crowd formed chanting, "Death! Death to the Christian!"

She pleaded for her life.

She was pelted with stones, punched in the face and drug through the streets. The local Imam finally intervened only to say, "If you don't want to die, you must convert to Islam."

The crowd descended on her again, beating her with sticks. Finally, the police stopped the attackers only to arrest her. For over a year now, Asia Bibi has been on death row for the alleged crime of blasphemy.

The war on Christians is not just abroad. It came to Boston just in time for the marathon, when two Islamic radicals blew up dozens of civilians. What perversion of the mind and soul makes a person capable of the random murder of innocent men, women and children in the name of God and religion? We will never understand.

Shortly after the attack, I met one of the Boston policemen who responded to the scene. He described his feelings as he witnessed the horror of a war zone. He described his sadness as he applied tourniquets and tried to save people. He described his anger as he helped pursue the bombers through the streets of Boston.

But he also described a special appreciation for American justice after the younger bomber was apprehended.

Trinity Church and Wall Street, 1914 lithograph by Rachel Robinson Elmer

He said, "We didn't drag him through the streets. We didn't beat him to death with tire irons. He will get a lawyer. He will get a trial. That's what separates us from them. That's the essence of the freedom our young soldiers fight for."

Some politicians hear of this war on Christianity and argue that we must fight a conventional war against radical Islam. I see things a bit differently. I believe we must defend ourselves against jihadists. We must actively use our intelligence capabilities to foil their terrorist plots and on occasion, such as Afghanistan, we may need to militarily defend against terrorists. But I see less and less likelihood that conventional wars and armies will defeat 50 million Muslims spread across the planet. Make no mistake, we should actively defend ourselves but the ultimate answer must come from Islam itself.

These Islamic republics see us as invaders and infidels. They will never accept us through force of arms. Somehow, though, they must come to understand that they must police themselves, that they must root out and destroy the sadists and killers who distort and contort religion to justify killing civilians and children.

Most Muslims describe Islam as a peaceful and tolerant religion, that at one time prized inquiry over the heads of infidels; the scientific method over fanaticism. I believe Islam still contains the roots of these classical traditions, and can return to them. There does not have to be a barrier to the tolerance, sophistication and advancement that once flourished in the Middle East.

President George H.W. Bush (left) and his son President George W. Bush, in December 2001 at Camp David.

44TH

BARACK OBAMA

2009 - 2017

I think my public service is part of that effort to express my Christian faith.

The young Senator from Illinois made history as the first African-American president. His father was born in Kenya; his mother in Kansas. Raised by his grandparents, he excelled in school and earned a law degree from Harvard. During his two terms in office, he attempted to fight high unemployment rates and a sluggish economy with massive government stimuli and increased spending. His landmark health care reform, colloquially known as "Obamacare," was aimed at nationalizing the health care system and expanding coverage.

Thanksgiving Day is a time each year, dating back to our founding, when we lay aside the troubles and disagreements of the day and bow our heads in humble recognition of the providence bestowed upon our Nation. Amidst the uncertainty of a fledgling experiment in democracy, President George Washington declared the first Thanksgiving in America, recounting the blessings of tranquility, union, and plenty that shined upon our young country. In the dark days of the Civil War when the fate of our Union was in doubt, President Abraham Lincoln proclaimed a Thanksgiving Day, calling for "the Almighty hand" to heal and restore our Nation. . . . let us rejoice in the abundance that graces our tables, in the simple gifts that mark our days, in the loved ones who enrich our lives, and in the gifts of a gracious God. Let us recall that

SECOND INAUGURAL ADDRESS
January 21, 2013

What makes us exceptional—what makes us American—is our allegiance to an idea articulated in a declaration made more than two centuries ago:

We hold these truths to be self-evident, that all men are created equal; that they are endowed by their Creator with certain unalienable rights; that among these are life, liberty, and the pursuit of happiness.

Today we continue a never-ending journey to bridge the meaning of those words with the realities of our time. For history tells us that while these truths may be self-evident, they've never been self-executing; that while freedom is a gift from God, it must be secured by His people here on Earth.

Michelle and Barack Obama at the African Methodist Episcopal Church, January 20, 2013.

our forebears met their challenges with hope and an unfailing spirit, and let us resolve to do the same.

—Thanksgiving Proclamation, November 23, 2010

Today and every day, prayers will be said for comfort for those who mourn, healing for those who are sick, protection for those who are in harm's way, and strength for those who lead. Today and every day, forgiveness and reconciliation will be sought through prayer. Across our country, Americans give thanks for our many blessings, including the freedom to pray as our consciences dictate.

As we give thanks for our liberties, we must never forget those around the world, including Americans, who are being held or persecuted because of their convictions . . . Let us continue to take every action within our power to secure their release. And let us carry forward our Nation's tradition of religious liberty . . . I join all people of faith in asking for God's continued guidance, mercy, and protection as we seek a more just world.

—Presidential Proclamation April 13, 2014

On our trip to Israel, Kelley and I were honored to be guests at a traditional Shabbat dinner on one of our last nights in Jerusalem. Sitting at the candlelit table, it was impossible not to feel the pull of centuries of tradition, ritual, history, and faith of the Jewish people. The meal began as our host said the Kiddush, a blessing to sanctify the Shabbat, and drank from the silver wine goblet. In front of him on the table, enrobed in an ornate cloth, was the Challah bread, its three braids symbolizing the command to observe Shabbat that appear in the Ten Commandments. As the evening progressed, I was struck by how joyful and exuberant the young men of the Yeshiva were as they sang in Hebrew and danced around the table. Their spirituality was just that, truly spirited. The older Rabbis, many wearing the traditional large fur hats, joined in the dance with clasped hands, and I was soon pulled into their dancing circle. While I'm not much of a dancer, it was hard not to get into the spirit of the evening! It was a moving and unforgettable experience for us both. One of God's greatest gifts to us is joy. Though the world we inhabit is not a safe place all the time, and though America today is being pulled by its leaders down the wrong path, I believe we must now, more than ever, find time for joy.

Conclusion

As I contemplate the quest to be one of our nation's leaders, I try to remember the stabilizing forces that keep me grounded in who I am and where I come from.

As I travel the nation, spreading a message of freedom and commerce, the long hours spent in airports and on planes and trains are sometimes a draining experience.

While our government definitely needs better leadership, our country also desperately needs something beyond the secular. Our country needs spiritual leadership and direction, because no amount of government will ever create a home or mend a broken family.

Some people have to go to church to see God. To me, it seems easier to see Him outside.

I look at the trees and the stars and I see His handiwork. The fireflies flicker and entice. They direct your gaze, encapsulate something fleeting, a feeling that accentuates something in nature more beautiful than anything man could ever create.

All around me, I see the mystery of God's creation.

But just as natural as it is to see God's hand in nature, I also find it natural and inevitable that man will doubt and question and search for truth.

Politics sometimes creates such blinders that the search gets ignored. Politics, at times, becomes so full of dead-enders with minds so closed that facts become irrelevant. They lose track of the search, if they ever cared to search. Easy answers, glib phrases and little left for the problem solver.

Is it any wonder that only ten percent of the people approve of Congress? The joke is—who are the ten percent who approve of Congress and why?

National Cathedral, Washington, D.C.

When I think of Congress, I think of Walker Percy's description of the search: "The search is what anyone would undertake if he were not sunk in the everydayness of his own life." The everydayness of life in Washington is that politicians are so caught up in the game of winning, of partisan plots and ploys, that no one seems to have time for the search. No one seems to have time for problem solving.

As a physician, I was trained to diagnose the problem and attempt a cure. In eye surgery we search for the visual obstruction and we try to remove it. In medicine, no one bickers for personal gain. There often isn't time for pointless delay. Physicians work together regardless of our political affiliation, regardless of our religious beliefs and mostly regardless of our personal differences.

Unfortunately, every good attribute of my medical colleagues is in serious deficit in Washington. In Washington, the atmosphere is so dysfunctional that even when we agree on an issue, we rarely can execute a solution. If legislation were a patient, we would still be fighting long after rigor mortis set in.

I think we face daunting challenges as a country and as a people. When I read the prayers of the Presidents it encourages me and gives me hope that our traditions, our belief in a Supreme Being, and our belief in the saving Grace of our Savior will help guide us toward a better future.

I want to be a part of discovering how we fix America, how we fix a broken spirit, and how we make America whole again.

The painter Robert Henri wrote: "Don't paint the material. Push on to paint the spirit." Reagan said "don't paint in pastels, paint in bold colors."

Several years ago, Kelley and I traveled to Israel with pastors, evangelical ministers, orthodox rabbis and just friends. There were about 50 people on this big bus and it reminded me of the church camp buses of my youth. I kept waiting for it to break down. It didn't, but we were almost washed away. It rained so hard we nicknamed the trip the "Flood Tour" and wondered what was next, plague or locust? About halfway from Jerusalem to the Sea of Galilee the road was literally washed out. We had to turn around and go back all the way to Tel Aviv. By the time we neared the Sea of Galilee we were all a little punchy. I knew we needed the mood to change. I told them to play some music.

We drove down into the valley of the Sea of Galilee, lush and green from the rain, with Guns and Roses' "Knocking on Heaven's Door" blaring from the speakers. It was perfect.

We all boarded a boat, some sort of old, wooden replica. It looked like something from the time of Jesus. Kelley and I both exchanged a worried look—wondering if we'd make it across. As if on cue, the winds began to blow and the sky darkened. What started out as a wet wind turned into a driving rainstorm. The boat began to rock sideways. It reminded me of New Testament storms that popped up from nowhere: "A furious squall came up, and the waves broke over the boat, so that it was nearly swamped" —Mark 4:37. Thankfully, we made it to the other shore. When we looked back, we could still see the rain falling halfway out into the sea, but there in front of the storm were two complete rainbows stretching over the Sea of Galilee. Our trip was filled with little miracles.

During that trip to Israel we traveled from biblical site to site and at each a pastor would give us a little homily or explanation of the significance of where we were. There is a terrific book called *Walking the Bible: A Journey by Land Through the Five Books of Moses* by Bruce Feiler and it reminded me of that. On the edge of the Dead Sea, surrounded by a forbiddingly harsh and rocky desert, is the lush oasis Ein Gedi. It's where David and his men hid out from King Saul, its many rocky caves providing him a natural refuge. As we gathered there one of the pastors in our group gave a powerful prayer ending with Psalm 18:

> *The Lord is my rock, my fortress and my deliverer;*
> *my God is my rock, in whom I take refuge,*
> *my shield and the horn of my salvation, my stronghold.*

Standing in that holy place, hearing that scripture read, I could feel the land beneath my feet and the inspiration for David's famous psalm, one that has sustained many leaders throughout our history as they seek discernment, wisdom and strength.

My fondest memory of the trip to Israel was standing in front of the Garden of Gethsemane. Like many others, I was introduced to my faith at a time when other things were much more important to me. But, as I grew into a man, and became a physician, that shaky foundation began to steady. As I stood in front of that garden of tears, the place where Jesus prayed and was betrayed the night before his crucifixion, I realized that I had walked my path to faith. I am a grateful loving husband and father. My God has given me the strength to be so. Though I need little else from Him, He continues to give me so much more—as He did that day at Gethsemane. I held Kelley's hand, and along with others we sang: "How Great Thou Art." Like the language of the communion rite of my youth, I didn't have to reach for the words.

Singing that hymn in the Garden of Gethsemane was powerful and it moved me deeply.

It is indeed a good day, any day, when we can listen and hear a song that sings so sweetly it stirs the soul. My hope for our great nation is that we listen and hear that song and that it guides us toward a better place.

For me, Christianity is not about being perfect. It's about being hopeful. God "pitched His tent among us" through Jesus who, from his humble birth to his brutal crucifixion, felt and understood human pain, fear and suffering.

Our spirits, bodies and minds may be broken but we know Christ's healing grace flows toward our weakness.

We are hard pressed on every side, but not crushed; perplexed, but not in despair; persecuted, but not abandoned; struck down, but not destroyed. We always carry around in our body the death of Jesus, so that the life of Jesus may also be revealed in our body. . . . because we know that the one who raised the Lord Jesus from the dead will also raise us with Jesus. —2 Corinthians 4:8-10; 14

Sources for Chapter Opener Quotes

Page 9: Washington's prayer journal, "Monday Evening," *George Washington, the Christian* by William Jackson Johnstone (New York: The Abingdon Press, New York & Cincinnati, 1919). **14:** Quote from a letter to Abigail Adams, November 2, 1800, the day after John Adams took up residence at the newly-established White House. **18:** Jefferson's First Inaugural Address, March 4, 1801. **23:** Madison's Seventh Annual Message to Congress, December 5, 1815. **27:** Monroe's Second Inaugural Address, March 4, 1821.**31:** Adams' Fourth Annual Message to Congress, December 2, 1828. **36:** Jackson's Fourth Annual Message to Congress, December 4, 1832. **38:** Van Buren's Fourth Annual Message to Congress, December 5, 1840. **40:** Address to Indian Council, August 12, 1802. *Governors Messages and Letters, Vol. 1 1800-1811*, Logan Esarey, editor, p 53. Copyright ©1922 by The Indiana Historical Commission, Indianapolis. **42:** Tyler's Third Annual Message to Congress, December 5, 1843**. 44:** Polk's Third Annual Message to Congress, December 7, 1847. **48:** Letter to Dr. Robert Crooke Wood from a camp near Monterey, Mexico, September 27, 1847. *Letters of Zachary Taylor From The Battle-Fields Of The Mexican War*, p 137. Copyright ©1908 by William K. Bixby. Published by The Genesee Press, Rochester, New York**. 50:** A Special Message to Congress, July 10, 1850. **51**: Pierce's Inauguration Speech, March 4, 1853. **53**: Buchanan's first State of the Union Address, December 8, 1857**. 55**: Lincoln's Second Inaugural Address, March 4, 1865. **62**: Johnson's Second Annual Message to Congress, December 3, 1866. **64**: Grant's Second Annual Message to Congress, December 3, 1866. **66**: Hayes' Second Annual Message to Congress, December 3, 1866. **68:** Garfield's diary, as cited in *The Road to Respectability: James A Garfield and His World, 1844-1852* by Hendrik Booream V, p 177. Copyright ©1988 by Associate University Presses, Inc. **70**: Arthur's Second Annual Message to Congress, December 4, 1882. **73**: Cleveland's Thanksgiving Proclamation, November 4, 1896. **75**: Harrison's Thanksgiving Proclamation, November 8, 1890. **77**: *William McKinley: Character Sketches of America's Martyred Chieftain* by Charles E. Benedict. From the Harvard College Library. Received from the Bright Legacy in 1880. **81**: Roosevelt's Fifth Annual Message to Congress, December 5, 1905. **86:** Taft's Thanksgiving Proclamation, November 15, 1909. **88**: Wilson's Thanksgiving Proclamation, October 2, 1913. **90**: Harding's Inaugural Address, March 4, 1921. **92**: Coolidge's Thanksgiving Proclamation, October 26, 1927. **94**: Hoover's Thanksgiving Proclamation, November 6, 1930. **97**: Roosevelt's Annual Message to Congress, January 4, 1939. **102**: Truman's State of the Union Address, January 7, 1948. **106**: Eisenhower's "People and Principles" speech, April 17, 1966. **111**: Kennedy's Thanksgiving Proclamation, November 5, 1963. **118**: Johnson's State of the Union Address, January 10, 1967. **124:** Nixon's State of the Union Address, January 22, 1970. **127**: "Gerald Ford: Prayer and a Quiet Faith" by Barrie Doyle and James C. Hefley. *Christianity Today*, August 30, 1974. **129**: *White House Diaries* by Jimmy Carter, p 399. Published in 2010 by Farrar, Straus and Giroux, New York. **135**: Reagan's State of the Union Address, January 25, 1983. **139**: Bush's State of the Union address, January 31, 1990. **142**: Clinton's State of the Union Address, January 19, 1999. **144**: Quote from an interview with Steve Scully of C-SPAN, December 18, 2008. **151**: Town Hall Meeting in Albuquerque, NM, September 28, 2010.

Sources

Page 14: Charles Francis Adams quote from *The Works of John Adams, Second President of the United States, with A Life of the Author, Notes, and Illustrations by His Grandson Charles Francis Adams, Volume 1*. Published in Boston by Little, Brown, and Company, 1856.**17:** Jefferson letter from *The Works of John Adams, Second President of the United States, with A Life of the Author, Notes, and Illustrations by His Grandson Charles Francis Adams, Volume 10*. Published in Boston by Little, Brown, and Company, 1856. **23:** *Letters and Other Writings of James Madison, Vol. II*, p 131. Published in 1865 by J. B. Lippincott & Co., Philadelphia. **29:** *Einstein: His Life and Times* by Philip Frank. Published in 1947 by Alfred A. Knopf, New York. **37:** Excerpt from a letter to Rachel from *The Papers of Andrew Jackson: 1821-1824*, Harold D. Moser, David R. Hoth, George H. Hoemann, editors, p 330. Copyright ©1996 by The University of Tennessee Press/Knoxville. **57:** John Hay quotes from *The Collected Works of Abraham Lincoln*, published in 1953 by the Abraham Lincoln Association. **59:** Quote from *The Lincoln Memorial: Album-immortelles* by Osborn H. Oldroyd, p 459. Published in 1882 by G.W. Carleton and Company, London. **61:** *Sketch of the Life of Abraham Lincoln* by Isaac Newton Arnold, p 73. Published in 1869 by John B. Bachelder, New York. **68:** Excerpt from *The Diary of James Garfield vol 2*, November 23, 1873, p 248. Copyright ©1967 Michigan State University Press. **73:** Quote from *The Writings and Speeches of Grover Cleveland* by Grover Cleveland, George F. Parker, editor, p 13. Published in 1892 by Cassell Publishing Company, New York., Daughter's account from *The*

Forgotten Conservative: Rediscovering Grover Cleveland by John Pafford. Published in 2013 by Regnery Publishing. **74:** Quote as cited in *The American Political Tradition and the Men Who Made It* by Richard Hofstadter, Vintage Books Edition, p 236. First published in 1948 by Alfred Knopf, Inc, New York. **75:** Letter to his wife as cited in *Benjamin Harrison: The American Presidents Series* by Charles W. Calhoun, p 21. Copyright ©2005 by Charles W. Calhoun. Published by Henry Holt and Company, LLC., Letter to a friend as cited in *Benjamin Harrison, Volume 2* by Harry Joseph Sievers, p 309. Published in 1959 by University Publishers. **77:** Quote from "Interview with President William McKinley" by General James Rusling. Published in *The Christian Advocate*, January 22, 1903. **107:** Quote from the *New York Times*, May 4, 1948., Billy Graham quotes from *Billy Graham, God's Ambassador* by Russ Busby and Billy Graham. Published in 2007 by HarperOne. ,*The Second Coming* by Walker Percy. Published on September 13, 1999 by Picador, an imprint of The Macmillan Group. **112:** Kennard quote from *Mississippi: A History* by Westley F. Busbee, Jr., p 282. Published in 2014 by John Wiley & Sons. **140:** Psalm 100:2, King James Version.

Permissions and Image Credits